CW01612673

Happiness, Truth & Holy Images

Happiness, Truth & Holy Images

Essays of Popular Theology and Religion & Art

John Thomas

First published, by Twin Books, in 2019

© John Thomas 2019

All rights reserved

ISBN: 978-0-9934781-4-7

The moral right of the author has been asserted

A Cataloguing in Publication record for this title
should be available from the British Library

The author can be contacted at: johnalfredthomas@aol.com

Cover: a servitor from Henry Wilson's Elphinstone Monument, University of Aberdeen (see *The Spirits About the Throne*), photographed by the author in 2014.

Made & printed in Great Britain
by 4edge Limited (Hockley)

Twin Books

Wolverhampton
PO Box 3667
WV3 9XZ UK

www.twinbooks.co.uk

Introduction

The little book – as it surely appears – is an eclectic collection of different kinds of pieces, culled from various sources. The religion in question, of course, is historic Christianity. Many articles here are ones which I have long had in mind, but came finally to write when, in 2018, I decided to produce this present collection (a perhaps-odd mixture of scholarship and speculation). Some are larger, re-written, versions of short articles which I have posted on my website *Affirming the Faith* www.affirmingthefaith.com Yet others, are revised versions of older pieces which, in many cases, were first written (and mostly published, in obscure places) in the 1970s and 1980s, and were, I hope, worthy of re-publication. Books by me, referred to here, are all available from the Twin Books website www.twinbooks.co.uk. Were there to be a dedication of this book, it should in fairness be to A. J. B. Higgins (I'm sure, however, that dedications need permission, and I would not know where to begin, with getting this one). My professor very briefly (New Testament studies?), in 1972, Angus once – commenting on an essay or some such – very quietly said "Of course, John, *you* have the gift of original thought". He could never have imagined the long, dispiriting decades, and dark despairing nights, that I kept those words beside me.

About the Author

JOHN THOMAS *studied theology in the University of Wales (Lampeter), history of art and architecture in the University of London (Birkbeck College) and the theory and history of church architecture and liturgy in the University of Birmingham. In 1994, his doctoral thesis* Theory, Meaning, and Experience in Church Architecture *was accepted by the University of Sheffield. For ten years from 1985, he was one of a group who produced* Church Building. The Magazine of Ecclesiastical Design. *He has also published studies of the work of Giles Gilbert Scott and John Singer Sargent, and written fiction, plays and theology. Fiction includes:* Department E *(2004),* The Welsh Dresser And Various Tails *(2009),* Beyond This Wilderness *(2011),* Not Long Now *(2012),* Death Tonight *(2013)* and Aubrey Annersley's Lucky Day *(2016). With plays and sketches, he has frequently performed his own material, including a short one-man comedy sketch (and once, dressed as a gorilla). Much of his work is self-published under the imprint* Twin Books, which he launched in 1999.

Contents

1 Happiness 8

2 Ecstasy, Art, & the Body. St. Teresa of Avila's 'Transverberation', and its Depiction in the Sculpture of Gianlorenzo Bernini 12

3 Actions & Reactions 17

4 Art & Saliva 20

5 Eternity's Paradox 21

6 Wagner's *Parsifal* 25

7 No *Fall*, No *Faith* – the Optimistic Doctrine 28

8 Oh *Really?* 31

9 Ghost Stories 33

10 Oughtism & Ought-Notism 37

11 Architectural Image and *Via Mystica*. St. Teresa's *Las Moradas* 39

12 Balance 49

13 The Spirits About the Throne. Henry Wilson's Elphinstone Monument, Aberdeen 51

14 Negationism. The Destruction of Western Civilisation 57

15 Orwell and the Sagrada Familia. Taste, Culture, & the Valuing of Church Architecture 60

16 Christianity & Beauty. A Few Words to Christian Aesthetes 62

17 Frustration Humour 65

18 Truth 67

1. Happiness

"Forget Happiness, search for ... TRUTH" are words seen on a notice outside a church by the eponymous hero of my short novel *Aubrey Annersley's Lucky Day* (2016). The quest for Happiness is everywhere, and indeed, the books that aim to guide people to it, and instruct them in it, are ubiquitous; they are authored by such well-known people as the Dalai Lama, various other religious leaders and writers, and of course, lots of others who are far outside any kind of religion: for happiness, in our society, is seen as the one necessary – and sufficient – goal in all of life, the one thing which we all should (and surely will) be searching for, the one thing that dovetails perfectly with any world-view, ideology, morality-system or value-set – or none (not that any of us actually have *no* 'overbelief'); happiness is the goal of other-worldly people and equally of purely-this-worldly people, of those of all political persuasions and of none, of the educated and the uneducated. Nobody really has to think about anything in particular in order to desire happiness. Parents may announce that they care nothing about what their children are or become, where they are from or where they may go, what they do or don't do: *as long as they are happy*. Happiness (at face value) is amoral and ultimately non-contingent, requiring – if you have it – no justification, explanation, or defence; it is a Holy Grail, and yet there is a wealth of people claiming to show you the way to it. Perhaps, however, there does not exist any actual definition of it (or again, some may suggest that there are too many *or* that such a thing is quite unnecessary).* It is not considered *unreasonable* to be uncertain as to what happiness itself actually *is*; lack of definition *may* be a virtue. Happiness is, in the last analysis, a feeling, an emotional state, a thing of inner experience (thus it is surely sovereign – if you claim to have it, no one can reasonably gainsay you – *your* happiness cannot be condemned as an illusion, and the idea that it may be in some way bogus must remain only other peoples' opinions). Therein – I consider – lies its problems (as well as its strengths); it is incapable of being a thing of objective knowledge, or a thing that may be falsifiable, and it may, like many feelings, be open to being manufactured by specific actions (but not necessarily inauthentic despite that fact). Of course, those guiding one to happiness, or guiding one's quest, may claim that the variety created by, say, drugs may 'feel' 'real', but not actually *be* so (they would be unconvinced of the 'no-gainsaying' rule, suggested above).

Perhaps a way forward is to compare happiness with 'contentment', and 'joy', since being psychological states, it could be said that there may be a superficial happiness (how I feel right now – on the surface, as it were), and my *underlying* psychological well-being (which I might call 'contentment'), and they are different things. Or, I might say (despite how I am superficially feeling at this moment) that I am overall 'fulfilled'. Fulfilment, or contentment, might come from the knowledge that I have the right career (and it is 'successful'), the right marital partner, or live in the right place (and, I might think, at the right time). Many would say that they seek *self-fulfilment, self-realisation,* or *self-actualisation*. These sound very good and laudable – except that it is difficult to be certain what they actually are, and if (or if not) they are realistic goals (such people might be following the words of Frank Sinatra ("I did it *my* way!")). 'Joy' may be a sudden, warm, psychological rush experienced when I receive, say, an unexpected present or honour – or it may be a deeper experience, of a kind that might be allied to contentment and fulfilment. The magnitude of the unexpected gift or honour will surely affect the duration of the feeling of joy; it may be something brief, or it may be life-changing, like my character Aubrey Annersley's big lottery windfall (particularly unexpected in his case, since he never bought a ticket in the first place).

Happiness, however, may be allied to *pleasure,* and 'the pursuit of happiness', we surely know, might just be, or might easily become, the 'pursuit of pleasure'; and the pursuit of pleasure can easily become the pursuit of *physical* pleasures, of temporary bodily sensations, of hedonism. For physical life has an intimate relationship with psychological experience. Superficial – everyday – happiness can easily be undermined by physical things – we may be at the mercy of digestion, bodily ailments, pain, or sleeplessness. All of humankind and society, all of life, is reduced, corrupted, brought down (despite temporary 'highs'), by the unnegotiable, fixed, and unavoidable nature of daily life, the rarely-relieved drudgery of quotidian existence. It is the experience of all of us much of the time, and pin-pricks of joy may come as brief contrasts to this gloom (indeed, the *contrast* might be the way these pin-pricks are created, and knowable). "But tomorrow" – C. S. Lewis somewhere wrote – "is a Monday morning", and *"Rarely, rarely, comest thou, Spirit of Delight!"* – Shelley wrote. The dreams, hopes and plans of political or religious utopianists always founder on the very ordinary realities of everyday life.

Oh yes, we all long for happiness, and those unexpected good things that may come to us, which, I have suggested, bring moments of joy; but they can be *very* temporary and unrepeatable, and they can too much depend on our *perception* of the things of the world around us. I once heard of a woman who read one of the many self-help/find-happiness books that are available, and it suggested pondering the amazing things of nature and the world, giving particular examples. She did exactly what was recommended, and did, indeed, feel uplifted. But as she said, the experience was temporary, and she would have had to read the book regularly to repeat the same experience, and *contemplation* (of the possible source(s)) was a necessary prelude to the experience; and surely, before long, the Law of Diminishing Returns would set in. The things of the world and nature are indeed wonderful – but only our *perception* makes them so (they are not wonderful when not perceived by humans, they just *are*), or makes them the source of a wonderful experience.

But if happiness, or otherwise, is a thing of personal psychological experience, maybe the nature or disposition of different people inclines them towards more or less happiness (or its opposite). I can think of a television presenter I often see, who is perpetually smiling, laughing and joking, and I often think, "I wish *I* was like that!"; and I know that there are opposite people, those who look to be permanently miserable – and my guess is that the events of those persons' lives have *not* caused the happiness or the misery they experience; perhaps, in truth, most people would fit somewhere between those extremes; and it may be that a joyous exterior ('sunny disposition') hides inner misery (and vice-versa).

Of course, we read often that Christians should be fully convinced of the joy and hope that lies in our free gift of salvation to eternal life; yes indeed, but we have to be perpetually *conscious* of that fact in order to benefit *psychologically* from it. 'Self-realisation' and the others, are, of course, inappropriate goals for Christians, since *self* is the key word there, and those who follow Christ are enjoined to die to self ('I did it God's way!' should be their epitaphs). The 'hope' thing I am generally sceptical about: we are often told that the Christian faith gives us 'hope' (I have near me a book of daily readings by Billy Graham, *Hope for Each Day*), but that isn't quite right – we don't have *hope*, but rather (agnostics ridicule us for this) the certain *knowledge* of the unearned gift of joyous eternity: but that (intellectual) knowledge perhaps rarely helps stave off the drabness of Monday morning. Rather, what we need to have – and such writings as those of Graham, and so many, many others, give us this – is constant recollection, remembrance, and meditation upon, this actually-present, but rarelyexperiencable reality; otherwise, we remain as fallen creatures – the Christian faith rightly tells us this – in a fallen world where there is rather less-than-we might-wish-for *delight*. And we might remember – as the church notice in the novel suggests to us – that if instead of trying to pursue *happiness*, you instead pursue *truth*, then happiness might come to you as a bye-product, as it were, unrealised.

* "... no one uses the word unhappiness these days, all deviation from the state of permanent bliss being considered an illness ..." – Theodore Dalrymple, *The knife went in. Murder and the decline of our culture. Memoirs of a prison doctor and psychiatrist*, London, Gibson Square, 2017, p.86.

2. Ecstasy, Art, & the Body. St. Teresa of Avila's "Transverberation", and its Depiction in the Sculpture of Gianlorenzo Bernini

It is some years, now, since I saw Bernini's famous sculptural composition commonly known as *The Ecstasy of St. Teresa* (1650s), in the Cornaro Chapel of the church of St. Maria della Vittoria, Rome. In this work, the central figure is a marble rendering of a woman, Teresa Sánchez de Cepeda y Ahumada, writhing in a state of religious ecstasy, which Teresa herself described in Chapter 29 of her (autobiographical) *Life* (1565):

> *Beside me, on the left hand, appeared an angel in bodily form, such as I am not in the habit of seeing except very rarely. Though I often have visions of angels, I do not see them. ... But it was our Lord's will that I should see this angel in the following way. He was not tall but short, and very beautiful; and his face was so aflame that he appeared to be one of the highest rank of angels, who seem to be all on fire. They must be of the kind called cherubim, but they do not tell me their names. ... In his hands I saw a great golden spear, and at the iron tip there appeared to be a point of fire. This he plunged in to my heart several times so that it penetrated to my entrails. When he pulled it out, I felt that he took them with it, and left me utterly consumed by the great love of God. The pain was so severe that it made me utter several moans. The sweetness caused by this intense pain is so extreme that one cannot possibly wish it to cease, nor is one's soul then content with anything but God. This is not a physical but a spiritual pain, though the body has some share in it – even a considerable share. So gentle is this wooing which takes place between God and the soul that if anyone thinks I am lying, I pray God, in His goodness, to grant him some experience of it.* – I have used J. M. Cohen's translation (Harmondsworth, Penguin, 1957), p.210.

- And when I saw the sculpture, that day in 1983, I was reminded of words of a theology lecturer of mine, heard when I had been a student (in about 1971), concerning Teresa's experience: "But of course, she was just having an orgasm, wasn't she?"; even at the time, though only about 20, I was aware that that judgement was surely somehow inadequate; surely, she wasn't *just* having an orgasm? Of course, the idea that Teresa had experienced some form of sexual, rather than religious, ecstasy, was far from new even in the era that had claimed to have 'discovered' sexual experience; such claims had been made many times, particularly with the coming of analysis based upon post-Freudian psychology, which, of course, has been applied to many things in religion, the arts, and beyond.

Inevitably, many people have poured scorn on Teresa's interpretations of her experiences, and naturally she has provided very fertile ground for cynics, sexuality promoters, feminists, materialist philosophers/psychologists, and writers of many kinds – and also (regarding Bernini's work) those who champion revisionist re-interpretations of Christian art; this is ground, one might say, which has been raked over many times. But those who do not have any animus against Christianity, and who seek to study Teresa's words – and the expression of them in art – from *within* Christian faith, inevitably look with very different eyes. Some have surely seen Teresa's experiences as having a purely spiritual nature; but the clue that this is not correct is found explicitly (unlike the idea of it being a purely sexual experience) in her own words. Throughout her many accounts, in the *Life*, of – very varied – religious experiences, Teresa creates, time and again, a hierarchy of the physical/spiritual nature of realities; this account, of her most famous experience, is no exception. She writes of the angel in *bodily* form, as rarely *seen* by her; *visions* of angels which she does not actually *see*, and, most dramatically, that she *sees* the angel stabbing her heart and removing her entrails with the aid of a sharp, burning object, which occurrence nonetheless did not cause her to bleed profusely and then expire. She explains: "... this is not a physical but a spiritual event ..." – but then she immediately qualifies it (" ... the body has some share in it ..."), and then yet again (" – even a considerable share").

However, when all the accounts of religious experiences in the *Life* are considered together, one slowly comes to doubt that Teresa actually has a very clearly-defined hierarchy, and certainly no reasoned separation between the natures of different kinds of things – but the same is true of accounts by Christian mystics from completely different times and cultures (eg. Julian of Norwich). She expends great effort in all her writings (and no doubt did throughout life), to describing and defining what we know as the stages or degrees of prayer (and in *The Mansions* (*Moradas*), the whole book is devoted to presenting a framework within which spiritual experience and ascent can be carefully explicated; but even here, there is on many occasions the cautionary note that the categories are not 'watertight', nor is any one experience divorced from another, nor must a strict, ordered *process* be observed/experienced). But what we can be certain of is that in her view, and experience, the physical and the spiritual – the bodily and the mystical – are *intimately* related. Whatever her experience(s) in the 'Transverberation' (as it is often known), it was much more than physical – but physical nonetheless (though not physical such as to cause the afore-mentioned wounding).

Of necessity, I personally have a great disadvantage in discussing the fullness of Teresa's experiences – that of never having been a woman, and thus never having had womens' physical experiences, sexual or otherwise. Experiences confided by Teresa's brother Lorenzo, however, are claimed to have involved some kind of sexual arousal encountered after prayer or after some kind of mystical event. This interpretation [1] is found in the account of Fr. Thomas Dubay, a scholar and authority on Teresa, in his book *Fire Within: St. Teresa of Avila, St. John of the Cross, and the Gospel – On Prayer*, Ignatius Press, 1989, pp.232-233. Also: *http://insightscoop.typepad.com/2004/2006/08/the_assault_on_.html*

He quotes Teresa:

> *"Pay no attention to those evil feelings which come to you afterwards [after Lorenzo's deep prayer]. I have never suffered from them myself, since God, of His goodness, has always delivered me from such passions, but I think the explanation of them must be that the soul's joy is so keen that it makes itself felt in the body. With God's help it will calm down if you take no notice of it. Several people have discussed this with me."* (taken from *The Letters of St. Teresa of Jesus*, Tran. E. Allison Peers, London, Sheed and Ward, 1951, 1980, letter 163, p.411 [Vol. 1]).

It has been said that love cannot flower, or be indefinitely prolonged, without some *physical* expression (the assumption, though, that this must needs be *sexual* expression is surely false); and perhaps the Lord's love of us is no exception. There is the physical element in worship, such as the physical expressiveness seen in liturgical dance, and the swaying motion, and gestures, often seen in Evangelical/Pentecostal worship, in which, hands held high and faces enraptured, a gathering is filled with the Spirit; worship, as seen here, is a bodily, sensual, experience. These, of course, are human expressions of love received – and love offered; but in the Sacrament, we specifically encounter the Lord's love of us, *communing* in and through that act (though, I would argue, it surely is, on many occasions, an event devoid of any special *feelings* whatever, and thus perhaps hardly seems to merit, to us, the label 'experience' at all). Can any authentic *communion* be devoid of *all* physical/material ingredients? And might it never be that the soul's "keen joy" might never make itself "felt in the body"? (And *how* in the body? – perhaps in many different ways). And if the nature of worship, and communing, is physical, perhaps salvation and eternal destiny are in some way physical also (one is reminded, perhaps, of St Paul's reference to an eternity, beyond the existence of this world, in which though we will have *spiritual* bodies (unlike now, where we have *natural* ("fleshly") bodies), they will be *bodies* nonetheless; 1 Cor. 15, 44).

Perhaps, as authentic religious experience *has* to be known, in this view, *by way of* the physical – this being the (only) form that humans currently have – aesthetic experience (whether we acknowledge it or not) perforce has to have a spiritual effect, 'spiritual' being defined as the non-purely-material part of the human whole (this, of course, assumes the view, now contested, that there is some non-material essence 'within' the brain/mind); this idea, of course, raises questions as to the nature of *spiritual effect* (and of the difference of *effect* between explicitly-religious art, and non-religious art). The mono-dimensional imagination, which the materialist world-view requires, means that such people (the 'orgasm only' variety) are unable to know both the partial-correctness of their approach (*physical* experience is indeed involved), as well as its sad inadequacy.

Such an artist as Bernini was from beginning to end a Christian person living in a Christian culture. To refer to him as a 'Christian artist' would have been a curious platitude. Such an artist would have been incapable of separating out his beliefs and culture – the whole of society's beliefs and culture – from his art; that particular – odd, tragic – dislocation is only a product of our own fraught age, one devoid of authentic belief in anything, yet clinging to the ever-cracking façade of – wholly groundless – belief in *ourselves* (to want to have Christian culture without Christian faith and the Christian world-view, is somewhat like the nature lover who might greatly value dolphins and porpoises, beautiful star-fish and whales – but detest ocean, sea: "We certainly don't want any of that great, nasty wet stuff!").

The Cornaro Chapel was constructed on the commission of Cardinal Federico Cornaro, Patriarch of Venice. A sepulchral chapel, it is a shallow space set in the left transept of St. Maria della Vittoria, a small Carmelite church [2]. Vital to understanding Bernini's work at St. Maria is seeing the space he produced – the chapel, with its architecture and sculpture, and painted vault – *as a whole.* To left and right of the sanctuary (beyond which is the space occupied by the sculpture) are two balconies, set high on the lateral walls; they remind us strongly of the boxes which are found in many theatres and opera houses; the sculpture's space, in this analogy, is the stage. Here, the well-known connection between Baroque art/architecture and theatre (the then-developing forms of oratorio and opera), is very apparent. The 'boxes' are populated with sculpted images of members of the Cornaro family (which included six cardinals, and Federico's father, the Doge Giovanni) who are meditating on the matter of the 'Transverberation', the image of which is *beyond their sight* [3]. Indeed, they are not actual spectators, since the image of Teresa, the rocks on which she lies, and the cherubim, are in a different space which is separated (and made inaccessible) by the architectural frame set in front of it – a veritable proscenium arch. The fact that the 'Transverberation space' is so completely separate, dramatically illustrates an important fact: the rest of us (as shown by the members of the Cornaro family, and their positioning) can only know of Teresa's mystical experience second-hand through reading of it, or seeing it through the visionary capacity of imagination (a quality that is very much present in Bernini's work), but cannot actually *experience* it ourselves. But what of the space that the Cornaros inhabit, or rather, look down on? It is the chapel's sanctuary; it is not the space beyond it (the 'Transverberation space') which holds the altar (and, presumably, tabernacle): we ourselves can receive the Lord's gifts to us in the form he himself commanded, the consecrated host, which is actually (though, as suggested, not necessarily an *experience*) a more complete and total *communion* than Teresa's powerful experience; and Teresa herself, in her *Life*, was the first to acknowledge that 'visions' were a lesser thing.

1 "One of the more surprising and disturbing phenomena that may occur during communion with the Lord is sexual disturbance or arousal. It is "surprising and disturbing" not because the phenomenon is in itself a cause for concern but because most people would never expect that in so holy an occupation there could be sexual repercussions. While they seem not to be common, they do occur. Lorenzo, the saint's married brother who had chosen his sister as spiritual director, had experienced these disturbances, and he asked her for guidance.", Dubay, work cited in text.

2 Howard Hibbard, *Bernini*, Harmondsworth, Penguin, 1965; 1978 ed., pp.128-141.

3 Hibbard,work cited note 2, p.130.

3. Actions & Reactions

Studying history – the process of trying to understand the past – is a very difficult enterprise. Any attempt to see the past, interpret it, understand it, and describe it, involves the fraught business of attempting to step outside of time, and see some century of vanished years without having one's own prejudices, world-view, assumptions, values (and, in a word, all that one consists of) distort and disfigure it; it is the business of trying, frantically, to derive objective knowledge and insight where, in truth, one is driven and contorted by *self*. We are all products of our time and society, and even if we reject its *mores*, shun the crowd, and tread the lonely path of counter-culturalism (Christianity, I believe, is just one thing that is of necessity counter-cultural), we can still only partially evade the world-view and values of our time. But in a curious – indefinable – way, this study, of past societies, is the only one that matters, the only activity that we may not choose – without risk, hazard – to avoid or disregard. How might we be able to see previous centuries, societies, people and things, while locked firmly within our *own*, without bringing many distortions? And trying to forecast the future – to guess it, more like – is even more fraught – for futurology is the one human enterprise that is bound to fail, or rather, the very best we can hope to do is construct a series of possible future scenarii, knowing that if one of our scenarii is found, later, to have had any co-incidence with the actual outcomes, the others will look ludicrous, and the one left will be no more than merely approximate, vaguely acceptable. And understanding our own time … perhaps that is the most difficult of all.

I have long thought of the present time – I mean my own time, the second half of the twentieth century, and the first decades of the twenty-first – as a massive *reaction* to the world of the late – Victorian/early-twentieth century era, which formed so much of modern life in my time, in Britain at least. Things that held strongly in the time of my parents (who were both born before World War I) have all been overthrown in the later-1960s, '70s, '80s, and up into the present time; they have been replaced, in so many cases, by the very *opposites*, in particular – I might mention – attitudes to patriotism and Britain's past, and to such things as homosexuality, race, and religion – but above all: sex. The ubiquity, and unquestionable sovereign power of sex, and all that is related to it, is – I can only attempt to explain and understand it this way – a massive reaction, over time, to the long-lingering power of Victorian prudery, or nineteenth century negative attitudes to sex, against which those determined to 'emancipate' us, strove so hard. And that Victorian ethos, and all its values and attitudes, was caused, in my view, by an equally-massive reaction to the extreme amorality of the eighteenth century world. Particularly, it was caused by religious revivals, which – as in the case of Methodism – were a direct response and reaction to the lax, slumberous, nominal religious faith of the Georgian age. Of course, many other factors operated at that time, particularly the agnostic humanistic philosophies of Reason, and the anti-clericalism (seen particularly, perhaps, in France) of the intellectual elites – that, in itself, is to be explained, I think, by reaction to the many centuries of European wars and conflicts concerned directly, or indirectly, with religion, or with differing understandings of the true nature of Christianity and the Christian church, which had begun with the Reformation – itself a massive reaction to the effects of the Medieval Church, and the sovereignty of the Medieval understanding of the true nature of Christianity. In the churches, much of the impetus towards 'liberated' theology is a reaction to the perceived, and actual, harshness of church leaders and their stern teaching in the past; and certainly this is true of the vast reaction of Western 'intellectuals' to the West's past – no longer a belief in the values and virtues of Western culture, ideas, and knowledge which justified their – admittedly, often harsh – dissemination around the world; now, we are also all supposed to have a kind of collective, and also personal, guilt, whose source, like all such emotions, is self-doubt and self-loathing; people in the formerly-subject parts of the world often do not have such things.

What I today find most curious and faintly risible is the so-predominant idea in these present times – perhaps each age has this – that *now* is *the* time, the time which the long processes of history (there is much belief, now, in inevitable *processes* in history) have all been leading up to; not only is *now* the time, but the idea is that things so beloved of today, and modern ideas and values, are the *right* ones, the right ones morally that is (and this in an age which thinks it has jettisoned morality!), and that they will – being right – be lasting, now they have finally arrived, for all future time. Somehow, people naively do not seem to realise that there will inevitably, sooner or later, be a reaction, perhaps a big one, to the mores of *our* time, in which our present ideas and values will be swept away, and perhaps considered quaint, if not reprehensible. The idea of 'modern' and 'modernity' have this fact built into them: what was 'modern' or 'modernist' when it was first conceived is perforce quickly of the past, and inventing ideas, and terms, like 'post-modern' will not help, since the things of postmodernity will eventually dissolve also. One process of reaction which I have often noted (and attempted to express in fiction more than once) is the inevitable (as I consider it) process from a thing being utterly proscribed – perhaps considered awful, by all – towards slow acceptance, liberation, legal status, equality with all other similar things – and then the slow (or perhaps fast) climb of the thing, whatever it is, to a status of superiority – *requirement* of it, perhaps – and thence to the effective illegality of that which once (truly) oppressed it. Somehow, things which have once dwelt in the shadows of oppression, once their legitimisation is conferred, are not able ever simply to co-exist, to be one thing side-by-side with the other, never, it seems, is live-and-let-live possible; *power* is the only destiny. Such processes, as suggested, may take centuries (the history of Christianity in Europe, and the Christian Church, is an example), or it may happen (as I think we have seen in my lifetime) very quickly. Many other things in our world can be perhaps explained as *reactions*; it is surely one factor behind the apparent fact of the legal/criminal justice system moving its concern to the reality of the perpetrators, rather than the victims: for long, any bias was clearly operating in the opposite way, and treatment of the convicted was harsh.

With political movements, such as revolutions, such a process certainly often occurs: revolt against an oppressor most often sees the rise of other oppressors (often the very people involved in removing the first oppressor), and the sorry, seemingly-inevitable rise of an oppression worse than the first; and, referring as I have to fictional depictions of the process, George Orwell's *Animal Farm* comes to mind as perhaps the best, most complete, representation. Why does it happen? Why do the oppressed become the oppressors? My suggestion is that here, again, we see the effect of the flawed, fallen nature of humans and humankind; if only, one might think, things were not ordered by *people*, then all might be well, or at least better than they currently are and always have been – but how could that possibly be? Who or what else would do it? While time lasts, perhaps the answer is *nothing*.

4. Art & Saliva

I've long had an idea ... and recently discovered confirmation, or at least an echo, in a rather unexpected place. I often find myself wondering about the origin of words where one idea or concept is derived or related (analogously, surely) from something completely different – or *is* it completely different? Just *how* has this come about (in each case)? In this case, it's the word *taste*, when applied to matters of artistic pleasures, or the discernment of particular good things from painting, sculpture, music, literature, and the rest. My idea, my theory, is that this particular use of the word *taste* had its origin in the fact, hardly realised by us, that when we encounter – perhaps unexpectedly – an art-work which gives pleasure, our mouth, and particularly the fluids in our mouth and substances related to taste and digestion, are somehow activated. For all I know, this is generally understood, by some, and obvious – but I have not read anything to this effect; until now.

In the third part (*Cities of the Plain/Sodom and Gomorrah*) of Marcel Proust's enormous biographical novel, or collection of novels, *A La Récherche du Temps Perdu* (*The Remembrance of Things Past/In Search of Lost Time*) the narrator has a long encounter (Part two, Chapter two) with the dowager Marquise de Cambremer, accomplished pianist, and lover of the works of Chopin, Debussy, and various then-modern painters, and he says: "Whenever [which, it seems, was often] she talked of aesthetic subjects her salivary glands – like those of certain animals when in rut – became so overcharged that the old lady's toothless mouth allowed to trickle from the corners of her faintly mustchioed lips a few drops of misplaced moisture. ... Secondly, if some overwhelming musical beauty was at issue, in her enthusiasm she would raise her arms and utter a few summary opinions, vigorously masticated and if necessary issuing from her nose." (Scott Moncrieff/Kilmartin translation, Penguin 1981, 1983, p.836). So, perhaps art does indeed give us some kind of oral, gastronomic experience. And here of course, as we might expect, Proust is connecting aesthetic experiences with sexual ones, animals "when in rut".

5. Eternity's Paradox

Long considerations of Christian theology, and living the Christian life, have inevitably involved endless thinking about *eternity*. What exactly is, or may be, *eternity*? Some Christians simply think of an 'after-life', which will proceed quite regularly when this one finishes, except that, unlike this life, it will have no end. Something 'beginning' (though endless) is perhaps the natural way that purely-time-bound creatures would conceive of it; but *eternity* is something different from that (we are, actually, incapable of conceiving of it, being purely-time-bound). It must mean something wholly outside time, and as such being in some way similar to the nature of the existence of God; it is *temporality*, we sometimes hear, that is the illusion. The reconciliation of human freedom of choice, with divine omniscience, is sometimes understood (well, attempted to be understood) by reference to God's existence completely *outside* time, and the Bible and Judeo-Christian tradition occasionally suggests the idea that God has created us "before the world [time?] began"; thus we, also, come from beyond time – for if eternity 'is' to be ours, it has always 'been'/always 'is'. This thinking produces some curious implications that are not often apparent, and might surprise, even disturb, us. It means, not only that we may well be 'in' eternity 'before' this life, but also, that we are 'there now' (as well as being *here now,* as we surely are – but not at the same 'time', for time does not exist in eternity; all these 'time'/'place' words are meaningless, of course, *in eternity*). Christian theories of Predestination and Election (coming from the time of the early Fathers, from ideas in the Gospels and the Epistles, and found in the theologies of the Reformers) perhaps began as attempts to grapple with this time/eternity paradox.

I remember that (in philosophy of religion lectures, in the early 1970s) we were asked to consider the implications of the situation 'if time was *real*' (looking back, I fancy one possible implication was that the 'evolution' of Truth, and much else, might be realistic). But if we accept the reality of present temporality (and I think we must), does it require us to believe that temporality is *all* that there is – if so, it might follow that this present life/the purely-this-worldly, is, indeed, all that there is. But *does* the belief that time 'is real' of necessity require the idea that *eternity* is an illusion? Eternity, I have suggested, is strictly inconceivable to us, and therefore – like the existence of God, I consider – an idea which we could not have thought of on our own, unaided, having (had) no means, or cause; no, God has put the idea of God in our hearts (Ecclesiastes 3, 11).

So often, however, the New Testament refers to the Kingdom of Heaven, a realm that will be established at some future time (or the place Jesus has come from, where he *was* with the Father); on occasion (as with the Incarnation), heaven breaks into earthly time. Many times, however, we find the New Testament suggesting that our individual translation to heaven is an authentically-future event which will be in some way dependent on our behaviour in the realm of temporality, and time and again we are promised eternal life/everlasting life as the result of believing in Jesus Christ (eg. John 3, 15); we may maintain the idea (suggested above) that eternity-thinking resolves the problems of free will existing with together with determinism, but paradox, I feel sure, remains.

Perhaps the references to 'heaven' should be interpreted as suggested above, as meaning eternity, a realm beyond time 'where' God exists, and such things as the coming of the divine 'son' were in effect the realm of eternity piercing, or impinging upon, that of temporality; heaven coming down to earth, as it does in the Gospels, was, by this account, just such an event. Certainly, the idea of an eternity somehow co-existing with temporality does help us, better than anything else, to approach an understanding of the nature of the Trinity, since 'God the Father' can be seen as the creating principle existing in eternity, the 'Son' as the temporal emergence of God (in the Incarnation), and the Holy Spirit being constantly present in the (temporal) realm (the world) while being a thing that is spiritual; all three, in Christian thought, are also somehow present/knowable within our own, material, realm; the Trinity, surely, *requires* some understanding such as this – and also such an understanding of the nature of God is necessary, I would argue, if God is to be truly-divine.

I am aware that these ideas about eternity and temporality, and the in-breaking of the one into the other (as in the Incarnation), are here written of in a very bland, simplistic, matter-of-fact manner (though many will of course dispute any *factual* nature!), and that this must contrast sharply, for some, with much else that is found in scriptures and in literature; but mysticism, and accounts of religious experience, are simply littered with references to a 'timeless moment', the 'intersection of time and eternity', 'revelatory moments', 'moments of vision', etc., terms both referring to those things of ultimate import (eg. as recorded in the New Testament) or those of many, many religious people, from a variety of cultures and traditions, in many centuries and places. Of course, all such references and experiences must never be disregarded or devalued – but there is need, I consider, to attempt to describe – although we can never *understand* – such things in readily-accessible language.

I fancy C. S. Lewis expressed the view that existing here, in the realm of time, was, when you examined it, an unnatural thing for people, who fitted badly into the world, and that we, Christians, inhabited an alien, occupied territory (he was probably writing in the 1940s, when enemy occupation of territory was a very real thing). Of course the dear Earth is our home (we should forget the current fantasies about future re-location in space) – but only while time, or *our* time, lasts. Is the existence – I would ask – of a co-terminous, but different, realm so very far from the scientific/science fiction ideas of parallel universes? (It often perplexes me that contemporary thought sees a water-tight compartmentalisation between ideas that are part of (or come from) religions, and those that are part of (or come from) science; many scientific people speculate about 'living forever' – and yet religious believers, we might consider, have that already.)

If we are created in eternity that, perforce, affects our relationship with the temporal world (and if we are created by God, as Christians believe, that perforce affects our relationship with our this-worldy parents). When I was very young (but obviously old enough to have heard of the universe, and space travel) I had the crazy notion that I had actually come from far, far away – some remote planet – and my parents were really sort-of foster-parents, who I had been assigned to (or them to me). Not long afterwards, I thought this to be mad, ungenerous, and *very* juvenile. Some years later on, I began to think that these childish notions were maybe not quite so silly after all … Soon after that, my own children were on the way (this was the very-late 1970s/early 1980s), and, as a result, I began to think about these things once again. My childish ideas were not so childish after all because (as I now consider) I (and everyone else, of course) actually came from somewhere that was *not* temporal Earth, but Eternity, and we were, are, really the children of God, created by 'him' as an intentional act, far beyond time's accidents. As someone about to become a parent, I realised that it was actually God who was 'sending' us someone, and that me and his/her mother had in fact no more than mixed the physical ingredients together; the child had existed *in eternity* as much as ourselves, and to eternity he/she (and all of us) would 'return'. Of course, however, our mother and father *are* our parents; but some time, whenever that might be, we will all return to our *true* home, and our true Parent.

The idea of eternity impinges on that old question of the dead, people formerly living on the earth. If you are a pure materialist, presumably you hold that such former-people have ceased to exist entirely, in that this life in the material world is the whole of existence, and that now, former-people exist only as chemical substances which they in some way return to the earth. Jehovah's Witnesses, I once heard, also have an essentially materialist view of things, considering that former-people do not exist at present, but will be re-created in the general resurrection that God promises. Spiritualists, presumably, are utterly non-materialists, and believe that former-people exist only as spirit-forms in a spiritual (but temporal) realm (along, surely, with other non-human spiritual entities). If, however, we conceive of a beyond-time realm called *eternity*, then human, former-earth dwellers, may exist in that realm, prior to a general re-making of them and their world in a future, different form ("a new earth and a new heaven") – indeed, ***they must*** exist there if, as I suggested above, it is outside time, and their existence is basically one eternal/timeless thing. Personally, I have never believed the idea (of spiritualists) that the entities made available to us in some form, eg. by means of séances, etc., are in any way related to actual people who have lived in the material world. They may well be real entities, but they were never granny; deception is surely their trade. The dead do currently exist, in my view, but not in any realm from which they may have any relationship whatever with us.

We are left, I believe, with paradox; we cannot simply evade and avoid such things. In the end, I think that we have – as so often in Christianity – to be content with, and live within, the tension between two realities: that which we ineluctably experience every day, and that which we cannot conceive of, trusting the God (if we believe in Him) who promised us – whatever it is – 'eternal life'.

6. Wagner's *Parsifal*

On the 12th of March 2011, I fulfilled an ambition to see Wagner's *Parsifal*; the production was that of English National Opera, at the London Coliseum. Sung in English (as is ENO's practice), this was in a production first staged by them in 1999, and directed by Nikolaus Lehnhoff (this production has also been staged in various cities in Europe and the United States).

Wagner's conception of the work seems to have originated in 1845, when he read Wolfram von Eschenbach's (medieval) poem *Parzival*, though his conception was much influenced by studies of Buddhism, and oriental philosophies, in the mid-1850s. Only in 1857 did he specifically connect his understanding of the story's themes with Good Friday, but it was 1865 before he took up the project again, completing the libretto ('poem') in 1877. It was a further five years before the opera was produced, at the Bayreuth Festival of 1882.

While the work borrows various ideas from Buddhism and Eastern thought (particularly renunciation) – the spelling with an S instead of Wolfram's Z was supposedly derived from the Arabic *Fal Parsi*, 'holy fool' – as it emerged, *Parsifal* was an essentially Christian work, or "ein Bűhnenweihfestspiel" ('A festival play for the consecration of the stage'), and the setting within the specifically-Christian-derived grail legends (as Wolfram's story), and the repeated references to the Lord and Good Friday, make it, in my view, a story whose Christian 'centre' cannot reasonably be denied (despite our necessary acknowledgement of the non-Christian ideas that contributed to its genesis).

Lehnhoff's production almost explicitly attempts to de-Christianise *Parsifal*; "This production of Parsifal does not seek to stage a sacred drama – a 'Bűhnenweihfestspiel'" – says Wolfgang Willaschek, in his article in the ENO programme ("Endgame in the Waste Land", p.27). Original productions set the grail hall of the grail knights (in which the mass/communion-like ceremony – or rather, benedicton – of the grail's uncovering is performed) beneath a cupola derived from a cathedral (normally identified with that of Siena). The significant act of destroying evil and its forces, in the story, was that of Parsifal making the sign of the cross with the recovered spear used at the Crucifixion. In this production, the grail and the grail hall – and the making of the sign of the cross – are omitted.

The de-Christianisation of Christian art is something I regularly complain about (the reason for it, in most cases, is that secularists/materialists can't produce their own art, so they have to distort religiously-inspired art to fit their agenda; besides, they can't write as good music; I have even heard of a secularised account of Elgar's *The Dream of Gerontius*, about as Christian a work as could be). The problem, with this production, is that though the traditional settings were radically replaced (and Wagner's stage directions seemingly ignored), the director went only half-way, retaining the words (complete with references to the Lord; I quite thought not to hear those), and, of course, the music. Thus, the libretto explicitly refers to meadows and flowers, etc. (throughout the work), but here, we were stranded in a sort of builder's junk yard, with fragments of concrete replacing the sung-about flowers; waste land indeed. If the stage directions were going to be ignored, why not doctor the words – as they were to be translated – to at least try to get the whole thing to make sense?

The community of knights, at Montsalvat castle in northern Spain, have charge of the grail or cup which collected Christ's blood at his crucifixion. The spear (used to pierce his side) has been captured by the grail community's 'rival', the sorcerer Klingsor, whose magic castle and garden are nearby, and whose ambition is to steal the grail also. Ancient lore predicts that evil can only be defeated, and the grail community restored from its current decline, when a 'holy fool' comes along, and destroys Klingsor's realm, and returns the spear. Parsifal (after an unimpressive start) turns out to be the 'holy fool' long waited for; but central is the curious female character Kundry. She is one of the most complex figures in literature (indeed, if we would find a character of such inner-contradictions, we might need to look to the characters of Shakespeare, rather than the world of opera). Kundry is a mixture of both the desire for redemption *and* the need to dominate and degrade those possessed of innocent virtue (particularly, that is, the holy fool Parsifal); she is both penitent and seductress, and as such is typical (or perhaps the prototype) of many late-nineteenth century *femmes fatales*. She laughed at Christ on the way to his death, and seduced various grail knights (including Amfortas, leader of the grail community), and she seeks, in Act 2, the redemption that she knows only Parsifal can bring her ... but urges him to spend just one brief hour in her embrace – which (they both know) will destroy them both eternally (and the grail knight's community also).

The notion that the barrier to redemption and virtue, is, supremely, *sexual* sin, is an idea crucial to many understandings of Christian thought, particularly, perhaps, in the nineteenth and twentieth centuries, and maybe formative of the ancient Christian traditions of asceticism. Thus, we have the dualist understandings of the opposition of matter and spirit which – deriving, one suspects, from Neo-Platonism – fuelled the search for spiritual purity in the renunciation of sexual physical life. From this ancient stream, surely, derives the idea that sexuality and holiness might be warring incompatibles. Of course, this is a distortion, mis-conceived, and while we might not be required to embrace a total rejection of celibacy, we must urgently promote the Christian valuing of physicality (whose acceptance might take centuries) when we have established a true distinction between distorted, degraded sexuality and the (perhaps hidden) virtue of its true, holy, nature. The real opposite of virtue is not sexual vice, but the rejection of the ultimate purpose of human existence (which is the abandoning of our pride before the reality, and experience, of God's love for us), which inevitably degrades our valuing of individual people, and thus ineluctably leads us to the materialist adoption of a vicious dehumanisation, which is the source of everything totalitarian and evil.

At the end of *Parsifal*, Wagner's stage direction makes clear that finally (the spear, and grail community restored) we see Kundry sink into lifelessness (redeemed, but dead). In the secularist understanding, of course, this is a very bad thing, since this present life is all, and there can be no kind of redemption that involves termination. In Lehnhoff's production, we see Kundry not expire, but rise and walk, with Parsifal, up a damaged railway track towards strong light (ie. walk off-stage). In fact, I found this rather beautiful, and, curiously, as authentically Christian as Wagner's original idea.

7. No *Fall*, No *Faith* – the Optimistic Doctrine

Harry Blamires's fictional character Canon Kirkbride relates a story about a piano-tuner visiting a street where every house has an old, disused piano, and *all* of them are out of tune, and need attention (this was the 1950s, when most houses in Britain still had a piano); (*The Kirkbride Conversations. Six Dialogues of the Christian Faith*, SPCK, 1958, pp.106-7). The point of the story is that the true nature of pianos – how they're meant to be – is *in* tune, and that being out of tune is not natural, not right; and pianos can mostly be returned to their proper state. If we consider – as the Christian faith teaches – that in this present world people are imperfect, damaged or flawed in some essential way, from their very birth, then there is the possibility that they may be brought back to how they should be, how they were always intended to be, *good*, as God first made them, and originally knew them. The reference, of course, is to the Christian doctrine known as Original Sin, or the Fall of Man (Kirkbride tells us that G. K. Chesterton considered that the doctrine should actually be known as "Original Innocence", since innocent was how people were originally created, before things went wrong, and Chesterton considered it to be the only Christian doctrine that could be *proved* to be true (*Orthodoxy*, Hodder & Stoughton, 1996 [originally 1908], p.10)). First made, by God, in a state of goodness, because humans, life, and the very fabric of the earth, is subject to the Fall; all are damaged, imperfect, and subject to decay and death (animals live mainly by killing, and even the seemingly-eternal rocks and mountains move, so slowly, towards disintegration; all is moving to its end). This is the fallen, crumbling world-of-death that we live in ... for the present, since the Bible makes clear that God will restore it to its first form – a new earth and a new heaven – and that, in that new world, there will be restored harmony (the lion now lying down peacefully with the lamb, etc.), the earth fully ordered and renewed, humanity re-made in its first form; and it was the defeat of death and evil, by Jesus on the Cross, that began this work, and made its eventual triumph certain. (Of course there is goodness in people, and order in nature – think of those shells composed in perfect mathematical form, or snowflakes – but that is only a part of the whole.)

But maybe there is a difference between innocence and goodness, perhaps goodness is a higher state, that of possessing the fullest, essential goodness of the Creator, rather than being simply a *tabula rasa* – and certainly, the final state of redeemed humanity will be of just this kind, a nature refined through the *experience* of fallen-ness, and the explicit acknowledgment and acceptance of Jesus' saving acts – our appropriation of them, our freely saying *"Yes!"*. This inherent imperfection is always with us, a flaw so true to our experience, so real to what we know of ourselves, of our constant inability to do only what we know is right; it is the perpetual presence of our frailty before relentless temptation (thus St. Paul Says "The good which I want to do, I fail to do; but what I do is the wrong which is against my will"; Romans 7, 19). Only by acknowledging it is there a possibility of our nature being changed, of the prospect of better things; thus our Christian doctrine is one of great hope, and hope leading to certainty, and certainty leading to transformation.

The alternative to this Judeo-Christian understanding is one which I fancy goes something like this: that all people are born in an 'empty', neutral state, like a page on which nothing is written, a computer disc on which there is no data recorded (the *tabula rasa* again), and all of our identity – one can no longer talk of 'nature' – is something acquired from other human deeds or actions ('nurture', not 'nature'). People become as they do, due to experiencing other human-instigated things, and thus badness of any kind is learned. Human institutions, systems, and ways of doing things, are (supposedly) the source; and thus, corruption of this original nothingness – one can't call it innocence – comes from already-corrupt systems-of-things – all of which were made by humans, since there is no other possible source of institutions, systems, methods, and the like.

Immediately, here, one sees the flaw, and it's the old 'chicken and egg' problem. How could any human institution or method be 'bad' *unless* it was created by intelligences that were themselves in some sense bad, or had an innate, unlearned, tendency to badness? Certainly there are evil human institutions and systems which damage people – but they only exist because they were created by *people*, and people who had a certain inclination towards bad things, an inclination which was of *no one's* making ...

People who hold this second, post-Christian, view are thrown back on the idea that by human effort, the bad institutions and systems in the human world can be changed, that people, as a result, can be transformed, and that – inevitably, eventually – the world will become a better and better place, and the final result – for our remote descendants – will be a largely-perfect world. But this humanistic doctrine – the most desperate, the most hopeless of all human sophistries – is the inevitable concomitant of the dark delusion that is materialism. Christianity, in my view, requires the doctrine of the Fall because if it should become, for some, a victim of their reductionism and naivety, they will perforce be left with this hopeless understanding of people – and will be left with a great amount of things that are inexplicable in Christian terms, and which only 'disappear' when thoroughgoing materialism is adopted. Rejecting the idea of a 'fall' leaves people with the 'I am what God made me' delusion, prompting me to do as my inclinations draw me (and seeing it as 'natural', inevitable, rightly unavoidable); and it is all God's doing, not mine, I am not responsible.

Every movement of fascism or totalitarianism that has cast its grim shadow on the human race has fed on the seemingly-beneficent illusion of mankind's present essential goodness; every dictator, with his death-camps and mass-graves, has been schooled in this pleasant-sounding lie – thus we cannot but sympathise with Canon Kirkbride's cry: "Take away the humanist's optimism, for it fills me with despair! Give me the Church's relentless insistence on our daily sins and our dyed-in sinfulness! It gives me hope." And we don't need to have obviously-evil totalitarian regimes to import all the ills that the 'essential goodness' fallacy will of necessity bring, since almost all of the ills and shortcomings of our present society, and its systems – education, criminal justice, politics, and more – result directly from this, and our rulers' bland assumption of it.

Of course, 'Original Sin' does not *sound* very nice; Chesterton's 'Original Innocence' not only sounds better, but is more accurate – and likewise, I contend, with my own suggestion: *The Optimistic Doctrine.*

8. Oh *Really?*

A long while ago, I chanced to see a documentary about Andy Warhol, and it included a short film, which was one of the many, I fancy, he made (I know little about Warhol; his art is really not my preferred kind). In the film, you simply saw Warhol sitting in an empty space, and heard a voice from off-camera making various statements, to each of which Warhol replied "Oh really". His intonations and verbal stresses were different for each statement, and they made it clear that his responses were one of questioning, irony, incredulity, and, occasionally, bland assent. This is much like my response to most things I hear – *Oh really?* – I say. Questioning, scepticism, and occasional downright incredulity is, I believe, increasingly necessary (but increasingly rare, sadly) in the modern world. This is not to recommend that we believe *nothing*, and commit ourselves to nothing – quite the reverse, as, being an orthodox Christian I believe that commitment to revealed Truth is very necessary, indeed, the only path to genuine liberation, and that the acid of *cynicism* destroys all hope; but I am perplexed when I encounter non-theists who have a bland assumption that questioning and scepticism are definitely not a feature of the lives of orthodox Christians; the truth is quite the reverse. As long as I can remember – well, from early-teen years, 50+ years ago – I have questioned, probed, reflected on ... many things, but mainly what I would now call 'ultimate things', things to do with eternal destiny, the meaning of life (perhaps, indeed, the meaning of the meaning of life), and at about fourteen I remember writing several stories about – a subject that fascinates me still – death. Often, from these times, I thought it ironic that I bore a surname recalling the 'doubting apostle', whose cast I was very much in. Even when choosing theology as a college subject (my 'Major', as the American education system calls it) I was aware that it could provide no career or even job; but there was no possibility of pursuing any alternative.

These were the times, of course, when a lot of things (received ideas in many areas) were being questioned, and this was particularly true concerning religious or theological ideas; professors and bishops were questioning and debunking almost everything, or rather, the things they were questioning were those of orthodox or traditional Christianity, and while I would claim, precociously, to have seen through their activities from early on, these were still interesting times to be living in – an orthodox or authentic (I might say 'comprehensive')

Christian faith, forged in these fires, was likely to be a lasting one (and so it has proved). Lasting, I feel, because of one important fact: namely, that questioning and scepticism (if *everything* is questioned) leads to (or is it 'back to'?) orthodox Christianity: Truth. Returning to where we started, and knowing the place for the first time, to paraphrase Eliot. Theology after all, and Christian faith, benefits greatly from those apophatic processes, which attempt to concentrate upon, and discover, the truths of the divine by pondering many negatives, by considering what God is *not*. (I didn't discover orthodox Christian writers, such as C. S. Lewis and Harry Blamires, till decades later).

Among the things which need questioning I fancy are anything – person, group, idea – that includes the word 'liberal', 'liberating', 'liberalism', etc. Are they really about long-term, *real*, freeing of people, or some short-term relaxation of rules allowing personal pleasures to be indulged? Another is today's tendency towards what I call 'Nowism' – this is the way it seems to be done by everybody *now*, therefore I'll just follow along ...

By questioning *everything* I mean to indicate the most important subject in need of questioning (and one which the 1950s-60s-70s theologians seem never to have risked approaching, let alone debunking): the whole *process* of questioning, and debunking, *itself*, and just exactly *where* their 'modern' ideas were actually coming from. By contrast, other areas of ideas seemed to have lived a charmed life also, perpetually ring-fenced by impenetrable harmful currents: the 'scientific' ideas, or ideas (unquestionably) assumed to be the products of impartially-acquired value-free objective knowledge. They were firmly off-limits to the theological sceptics. Today, we see more clearly (well, some of us do) how our world is increasingly ordered by things which are actually ideology, or politics, dressed up as science, and carefully attired thus so that they rest *virgo intacta* within the unquestionability fence – global warming is such a thing, as is evolutionism (not to be confused with *evolution* itself*; most people assume only the ideology, and neither know nor care about the development of kinds of life). Of these, and other materialist/this-worldly ideologies and processes, my reaction is: *Oh really?*

* See my *Christianity and Materialism. The Church and the World in Western Society*, Twin Books, 2015, pp.16-18, etc.

9. Ghost Stories

I *love* a good ghost story – sitting with kindred spirits around a roaring fire, perhaps at Christmas time (or at least when it's dark outside), a comfy chair beneath me, and a glass of port in my hand, and a nice, kind man – perhaps white around the temples, bald in places – recounting events from long ago, when, travelling far and wide among the ruins of venerable civilisations, garnering mysteries and disturbing tales, he ... And then there is the moment of delicious unease that slowly creeps upon one, spine-tingling, perhaps, unnerving, leading, finally, to a climax of ... pure ... terror ... What, oh what, could be more satisfying! (But don't ask me *why* ...)

Recently on television, we have been treated to a re-run of Mark Gatiss's 2013 documentary about that legendary writer of ghost stories, the Cambridge academic M. R. James (1862-1936), and the repeating, also, of several James stories, including one directed by Gatiss himself (the James stories were originally told by their author, at Cambridge, in precisely the kind of setting I've attempted to describe). I'm sure I saw all these programmes the first time around, but was keen to see them again. I have a book of the stories somewhere, and books of other horror/creepy stories by other people, from the well-known, such as Poe, Dickens, and Henry James (*The Altar of the Dead*) to the less-well-known; and Agatha Christie's *The Last Séance* is about the least-pleasant story I know of (no cosy village biddy in this one, shrewd or otherwise). And, as you might expect, I often think to write a ghost story myself (I do, after all, write stories – two or three a year, at the last count). Unfortunately, I always seem to be stymied, stumped, brought up – but slowly, not fast or hard – against reality, the way things really are, which is what, I consider, writers *should* be writing about (however pleasant a little falsehood or two would be). Spirits and demons of the literary (and, of course, filmic) variety are not *quite* real. People who write a story – or produce a film, play, graphic novel or even computer game – have to do just that, I realise, produce a *story*, they have to engage readers; but once you draw, for your subject-matter, upon evil, you need, I consider, to have an idea (exact, or at least vague) of what evil actually is.

No, I'm not going to give a preachy this-worldly remonstrance that 'evil' is just bad people who do awful things, like bombing shopping centres, killing elephants, or spreading bad ideas like racism, and that all those supernatural things found in ghost stories don't really exist; no, being an orthodox Christian I believe firmly in a spiritual realm, which exists around and within the material one we directly know. It is the habitat of a vast wealth of entities, of many different kinds (including morally), and hierarchies, and varieties of organisation and intent. Such beings (or at least, the malevolent ones) are the entities found in our ghost stories and horror films. The stories, films, plays and the rest, are, indeed, *full* of them – but do their originators really believe in the existence of such things? I wonder this, but I suspect not, for I consider that most people in our society today (certainly those whose work fills the media, and the places of power and influence) are thorough materialists (materialist in that they think – indeed, feel certain – that everything that exists has come into being by chance, impersonal, undirected processes, and that this life, and the material realm, is the sum total of existence, and all that there ever will be). Such beliefs, above all, are very comforting, for they remove the dread possibility that we all may one day be subject to something above and beyond ourselves, something we cannot ourselves control, or even rationally discover; death – extinction – is far less awful than that. Of course, for some of such people, the 'pull' of ghost stories *may* be that their subject matters may seem to offer a part-subliminal questioning (and answering?) of their materialist assumptions (if so, I suggest that a corrective reading of Darwinism – which *claims* not to be fictional – will quickly cure them).

Yes, the *real* spiritual realm, and the activities of its inhabitants, are rather different, in my view, from the stuff we (mostly) find in stories and films. Leaving aside the visual media, we have things made of *words* – we have nought else – and the words found in ghost stories would, I fancy, include such as: dreadful, fascinating, chilling, spooky, unease, curiosity, mystery – and others; 'awful' and 'awe-full' would, of course, figure prominently in such a list – but these are very complex words, requiring a long explication of their own (even more so 'numinous' – and also 'Gothic', which only had its modern connotations of the dark and dreadful since the 17th century).

No, the person who ignores the reality of spiritual evil may one day come to regret it considerably (or one who attempts – and this is worse, I think – to 'rationalise' it, or translate things into purely-human terms). I have known Christian deliverance ministers (also known, inaccurately, as 'exorcists') who have struggled with 'men' who have developed exceedingly super-human strength, and chaotic anger and violence, when the name of Jesus is mentioned; a young woman who wept as she recounted a hideous satanic ritual that was forced upon her (no, it wasn't 'just about sex'); a woman who for years – while having much attention, and care, from deliverance ministers – struggled with a malevolent spiritual presence within her (also known, also inaccurately, as 'possession'; in reality *she*, despite her loathing of it, in a sense possessed the thing, not the other way round). The materialist assumption quickly turns these things into mental illness, hysteria, and a variety of complexes and pathologies. Of course such illnesses do exist and harm people; but to see reality in terms of one kind of thing alone is to attempt foolishly to see reality through narrow, unimaginative eyes that will look at one dimension only, it is *nothingbuttery* and reductionism of the most feeble kind; of course there is mental illness, but there is also something else. It is common (particularly, I fancy, in religious circles) to claim that to understand evil as being somehow connected with non-human beings is an evasion, an unwillingness to see humanity as it really is. I (as is usual with me) see it the opposite way: that the evasion is theirs, since not having to commit oneself to non-material things is much more comfortable (except commitment to belief in the nice things, of course, the things one would want to have).

The reality of spiritual evil, I would suggest, is not the stuff of stories, because it is not anything to which the above words could be applied. Rather, encountering it and its agents is a rather dark, grim affair; it is not fascinating, but boring, not so much awful as deathly dull; words we might use would include: colourless, hopeless, lifeless, broken, drab, despair, regret, emptiness. Things of evil promise much (most satanists, I've read, worship nothing; they're only in it to acquire power) but deliver only death, obliteration. None of which make a good story. But do *ghosts*? Mark Gatiss recalls the question that M. R. James, like most ghost story writers, was inevitably asked ("Do you believe in ghosts?"), but he fails, like most people concerned with these things, to ask (or say if James asked) the question that must hang in the air above us: What *is* a ghost? I firmly believe that the real inhabitants of the spiritual world are not, and never have been, anything to do with formerly-alive people (despite the many, many claims made to the contrary, some by humans) or our dead forebears, dismally waiting in some dreary place until a desperate descendant calls them hither, perhaps with the aid of not-disinterested agencies of dubious intent.

I must confess that I have myself written a novel which proceeds from the Gothic (the real Gothic, though, the beguiling remnants of half-understood ancient ruins, within and among worldly, slumberous Georgian Christianity) – but ends with the reality of spiritual evil, and the (only) means of its defeat (*Beyond This Wilderness*, 2011), and also a modern-day story concerning such things (*Billyriddle*, 2009). But should I write more, suspend belief, and attempt to describe dark, silent watchers, threatening figures upon an empty shore, rampant, writhing, bed-sheets, and curious dust floating in time-locked libraries ... ? Well, maybe – might go down awfully well next Christmas ...

10. Oughtism & Ought-Notism

Somewhere, C. S. Lewis refers to the matter of St. Augustine and un-baptised babies. As 'everybody knows', Augustine believed that such babies go straight to hell. But we are not entitled, Lewis says, to suppose that Augustine – if he really did think that they did – was happy with this fact, or believed that it *ought* to happen. Instead, Augustine took his beliefs from scripture, reason and other sources, other, that is, than what he believed ought or ought not to be the case. So many people today don't think like this. They are happy to believe a variety of things which, if examined, turn out to be a collection of what they think things ought or ought not, should or should not, be true.

The 'hard', or seemingly-hard, sayings of Jesus are quickly dismissed, along with any reference to God's judgment, because of course, such things *ought never to be allowed*, and therefore – the logic goes – they can be made not to exist, simply by thinking them out of existence. Oughtism – perhaps a lot of it should actually be called *ought-notism* – can be found everywhere, even in churches. Oughtism, of course, is a product of that curse of our age, postmodern subjectivism, the mindless (lack of) thinking which causes otherwise-seemingly rational people seriously to believe that *their* 'truth' is just as valid as the next person's, however different, and that whatever they choose to believe can simply be real, while not affecting the next person's 'truth'. The reasonable person does not believe such things for a moment, and honest people accept that however things *are*, in reality, they will probably not be ordered as they are by anything that you or I care to think about them.

A lot of Christian oughtism is based upon belief in the total and utter nature of God's love for us. God is love, that we know, and his love can result in absolutely anything. Thus oughtists are quite certain to be sceptical about ideas of what God has not allowed, or has required, in all the traditional formulations of law and morality. Because God loves us *so* much, he cannot have really proclaimed that we *cannot* do *that*, or *must* do *this*, he cannot, would not – this thinking goes – ask us to act against *our nature* ... and they fall readily into the mistake of believing that God has made us as we are, failing to understand the world we live in now.

Such people, like all oughtists, replace any notion of God that we find in scripture or Christian tradition, with one of their own making; because *I* would not require such a thing – it *ought* not to be required, in my view, then neither ought God – who is promptly re-made in my own image. And oughtists readily fall into the trap of believing that humans are originally, inherently *good* – because, of course, that is how they *ought* to be, how we would all like them to be, how things *should* have been ordered ... and hence they arrive at the opposite of the Optimistic Doctrine ('Original Sin'); the road to hell, they quickly forget, is paved with the *very best* of intentions.

Oughtist Christians are very tiresome, almost as much so as oughtist Humanists and Materialists; both choose to escape into the world of wishful thinking, but once having done so, they are often apt, sadly, to look down from their moral high-ground upon the rest of us with a certain disdain.

11. Architectural Image and *Via Mystica.*
St. Teresa's *Las Moradas.*

Las Moradas is unusual among mystical writings for its use of a sustained and complex physical image, an image which at the same time is the structural organisation of the book, and the schematic organisation of the spiritual process which is the work's chief concern. Written in 1577 by the Spanish mystic Teresa of Avila (1515-82), *Las Moradas* is usually translated *The Mansions*, but is often known by the excellent title *The Interior Castle*[1]. It was written at the insistence of her religious superiors, and its intended audience was the sisters of the various convents which the saint founded and oversaw.

The writer asks us to imagine a great castle or palace or mansion which has seven parts or zones. These areas are not placed one after another, along an axis, such as a series of bays or courtyards, but are concentric, like the "many layers of bark on a palmito tree"[2]. Each of these mansions is not one physical entity, however, but is itself a collection of spaces, hence each is called 'first mansion*s*', 'second mansion*s*', etc. The great complex building, or series of buildings, is an image of the soul. The religious seeker after truth must journey into this building by degrees, the soul having its fullest being or residence in the Seventh, the final mansion. Such a person must thus enter unto herself, and St. Teresa is aware of the problems associated with such a suggestion[3].

A second meaning is involved at the same time, however: the mansions are the dwelling-place of God, the palace of a divine king, and as the first few mansions are the outer courts of this royal residence, so the Seventh is his private inner-chamber, the place where he can be truly known. The two meanings are not merely piled one on another, but are to be understood together – God takes his pleasure, we are told, in dwelling in a pure soul; at the core of the innermost mansions God and the soul have their discourse[4]. The whole structure is vast and intricate, and involves different levels, or kinds, of spiritual life:

> *"Thus this palace has around it many rooms, and the same above, because the things of the soul have to be considered in their fullness, breadth ... and grandeur, without fear of exaggeration, because the soul's capacity is greater than we imagine, and in its every part the light of that Sun, which is within the palace, is diffused ..."*[5]

The difficult journey of entering into one's own soul is to be achieved by one means of passage: prayer[6]. The journey is not described in terms of any allegorical story, such as Christian's journey in *The Pilgrim's Progress*, but by means of a description of the different kinds of prayer, or stages in the process of mystical union, the *via mystica*. These stages are also described in her other works, and basic classifications of prayer and meditation are found in different forms throughout Western mystical literature[7]. Different parts of the journey are completed with varying degrees of ease and difficulty: the first few mansions are quickly moved through (by a spiritual adept), but then come the obstacles – the Devil and his minions – which rather increase as each new mansion is entered[8].

The physical image, our main concern here, is used at various levels, assuming more importance at the beginning, but never being abandoned. From what source did the saint acquire the image? Certainly, the germ of the scheme goes back to 1565, when she wrote *The Way of Perfection*, but it was the vision of 1 June 1577 (when the castle appeared before her in a crystal sphere) which inspired the work itself[9]. One possible starting point, or origin, was St. John 14:2, "In my Father's house are many mansions" (AVKJ)[10]. The Latin Bible, the Vulgate, had *mansio*, 'halting place' 'lodging', 'inn', and the Greek behind *mansio* is *monai*, 'stopping place'., 'station'[11]. C. K. Barrett tells us that various ancient and modern writers understood the verse as implying progression in the heavenly life; this is false, he claims, as shown by the use of the same word in v. 23: "Anyone who loves me will heed what I say … and we will come to make our *dwelling* with him" (NEB) – the word refers, that is, to a *dwelling*[12]. For St. Teresa, the understanding of the "many mansions" as a *dwelling* is clearly crucial. At the same time, the meaning involving spiritual progression, similar to that mentioned by Barrett, is clearly relevant to St. Teresa's use, and such a reading of St. John 14:2 may have been within her understanding; again she appears to be employing multiple meanings simultaneously.

This idea from the Fourth Gospel may have been the source of the actual imagery employed, but a possible source for the greater scheme is the mythological realms or spheres of Dante, which could have been well-known to Teresa. A source of Dante's scheme nearer home was *El Laberinto de Fortuna*, written by the Spanish poet Juan de Mena in Seville in 1496. This is a mixture of theology, astrology, and world history, and involves three concentric realms (past, present and future) through which the poet is guided by a Beatrice-like beautiful woman, 'Divine Providence'[13]. The poem is in seven parts, and the significant number seven derives from the Ptolemaic planets (Dante's nine heavenly spheres involved these plus two others)[14]. As the title of the Spanish work suggests, these two, and many others, are products of the great chain of stories based on the myth of the underworld or labyrinth journey. The labyrinth was a real structure in ancient Egypt, which was excavated in modern times, but the most significant mythological connection is with the Cretan labyrinth, the setting of the story of Theseus and the Minotaur. From early times, labyrinth myths were represented graphically by a two-dimensional diagram which later produced the turf maze (sometimes known as a 'Troy Town')[15] and the hedge maze; the Tudor knot garden may have had a common origin[16]. Some of these, like children's puzzles, involved a series of false trails and dead-ends, with one true route leading to the centre. Others, simply consisted of concentric circles or squares. Such diagrams were set in the floors of churches from the Patristic period to the Middle Ages. That at S. Maria di Trastevere, Rome (c. 1190) has concentric rings enclosing nine regions, and has been compared to the degrees of beatitude, by which the soul approaches heaven, as in Dante[17]. It is difficult to draw any general conclusion on the origin or significance of the labyrinths and mazes, however. The early stories of labyrinth journeys have been demythologised as explanations of the nightly death, and daily rebirth, of the sun, which spends the dark hours overpowered by evil in the great labyrinth under the earth, to emerge triumphant each morning at the labyrinth's eastern door[18]. These diagrams have been seen as representations of heaven, or specifically, of the heavenly bodies[19]. Spiritual interpretations connect the diagrams with the Fall of man, the loss of contact with the sprit, and the need to find a way back to the centre of being, or the remoteness of life from its subconscious fount[20]. This approach naturally has similarities with the theme of *Las Moradas*, and the book is surely to be seen in this context, having an archetypal link with these myths and their scheme. A simple diagram of concentric rings could easily represent it[21].

However, St. Teresa's degrees or states of mystical experience do not precisely fit the number seven (or nine)[22]. Her use of seven was no doubt in conformity with tradition. Medieval writers and ecclesiologists were obsessed with the magical properties of numbers, a concern ultimately inherited from Pythagorean numerologists, by way of Neoplatonism and the Fathers of the Church[23]. Twelve was a key number, but seven was even more important, it was "regarded by the Fathers as mysterious above all others" and it "intoxicated the medieval mystic"[24]. It was the sum of four (the number of the body) and three (the soul)[25]; it is the number of humanity and "expresses the union of Man's double nature. All that relates to him is ordered in series of sevens"[26]. Its use and importance was no doubt linked to the Ptolemaic system, as mentioned above[27], and St. Teresa's use of the number probably reflects the lingering of these ideas.

The *Moradas* may also reflect an intellectual system which was fascinated with the esoteric approach to religious buildings and their symbolism. It seems that there was much speculation in sixteenth century Spain concerning the nature of the Solomonic Temple at Jerusalem. A reconstruction of it was made by the Jesuit Juan Bautista Villalpando, later published in his commentary on Ezekiel (1596-1604), and this seems to lie behind the schemes for the Escorial, Philip II's palace and monastery complex, near Madrid, designed and built in the years 1562-82[28]. It is hard to ascertain the precise degree to which numerology and arcane lore influenced the planning of this building. It has, however, been suggested that the design of the precincts was significant (as at the Temple), and involved seven courtyards[29].

St. Teresa's castle is above all a building for some kind of residence, it is a house. It may be the palace of a king, or the dwelling-place of a soul, but it is nonetheless a domestic building. This is significant. Houses are in most cultures, particularly primitive ones, the most important buildings; for some, indeed, they are sacred. Many religious architectural forms have the idea of the house behind them. Most common is the idea of the special dwelling-place of god on earth, the divine locus: the temple as *domus dei*. Also there is the concept of the true home or dwelling-place of a sacred body of believers or initiated sect (in Christianity, the *domus ecclesiae*). In certain societies, houses are valued even today as places in which a person can live in absolute privacy, the suggestion being that only within its walls can the person truly exist in the fullest way[30]. So often we hear of thinkers and contemplatives locking themselves in inner chambers, there to enjoy inner experience, as though it were impossible elsewhere, as though the inner place into which they desire to go somehow relates to the inner space which they physically inhabit – and here we are back to the mystic's journey into the interior castle of his own soul. The house may indeed be likened to the deepest part of the human mind, which would easily explain the use of domestic images in writings, and the importance people place on their homes. Olivier Marc tells of his feeling that the idea or concept of space exists somehow within us, and that the act of experiencing spaces in buildings is in some sense a re-living or re-discovering of what is already there, and always has been there, in the subconscious[31]. Space is experienced interiorly, to put this notion into St. Teresa's terms. Marc, in his effort to explain this idea of his, looks at the origin of the house, and decides that the first dwellings, being built without any kind of pattern or precedent whatever, were an unconscious externalised image of the womb, which is the origin of the idea of space, fixed deep within us[32]. To modern man, the possible connection between the womb and a private retreat is well understood. Each person, it is held, is unwillingly expelled from the womb, and dreams of return, and if the connection between this inner world, and the 'artificial' home made by man is true, then it is easy to see the power and source of architectural images, particularly in a spiritual context.

Architectural images play many different roles in literature of all kinds, of course, and in different kinds of religious writing. Here, in *Las Moradas*, we have it used in connection with spiritual process, or progress on the spiritual journey. It is not, however, connected with the spiritual condition of a particular person, nor a kind of symbolic Everyman, but it is rather objective and practical. Also, the image is not used to convey any basic theological truths about the nature of man, as such images can be used., it is not the exposition of a theological system (or religious understanding as such), and there is no specifically didactic role[33]. The frequent use of architectural imagery for religious writings is strong testimony to the power of great architecture upon the mind and imagination of man, even if deeper urges do lie beneath that power. An architect must be a visionary in order to conceive something, then construct it, but always the construction falls short of the vision. Great buildings also convey greater visions to the imagination of some of the persons experiencing them.

For St. Teresa, however, the architectural image of the great palace is only a device; there is no suggestion that physical buildings play any part in the process of the union of man and God. (The mansions are not used as an actual means of describing the states of religious experience themselves – the image remains external to the experiences being described.) However, buildings are, as we have seen, pervasive, and diverse in the part they play, in this brilliant work. The framework provided by this schema helps to prevent the writer falling into the familiar seemingly-formless wanderings that bedevil so many mystical works. Though the 'mansions' schema, as we have seen, remains throughout, it is finally transcended, just as language itself finally ceases to be able to describe experiences which are of their nature indescribable.

1 *Morada* can be translated 'mansion', 'habitation', 'abode', 'dwelling' or 'sojourn'.

2 1st Mansions, Ch. 2.

3 1st Mansions, Ch. 1.

4 1st Mansions, Ch. 1. Again the saint talks of a building as the "great and precious edifice" of the soul (2nd Mansions), and the *The Way of Perfection* (Ch. 30) describes "a pure soul adorned with virtues" as "a beautiful building".

5 1st Mansions, Ch. 2. I have used the translation (made by "a discalced Carmelite"; 1944) re-issued by the Catholic Publishing Co, South Ascot, Berkshire, n. d. (1960s?).

6 "The door by which to enter this castle is prayer" (2nd Mansions). Evelyn Underhill, presumably quoting from the *Life*, records St. Teresa's comment that her prayer "began to be solid like a house" (*The Mystics of the Church*, 1964 ed., New York, Schocken Books, p.174). The other great Spanish mystic, St. John of the Cross, uses a fleeting architectural image in his key poem *En Una Noche Oscura* ('On a Dark Night'), describing his ascent of a secret staircase, above a silent house, to meet his divine lover. The staircase is a particularly evocative physical image, vividly depicting the spiritual ascent from earth to heaven to higher planes of consciousness – with Biblical precedence, of course.

7 F. C. Happold divides the 'mystic way' into three stages: the Way of Purgation, the Way of Illumination (*or* the Illuminative Life *or* Proficiency *or* Contemplation) and the Way of Union (*or* Unitive Life). This is just a "rough diagram", however, as different mystics give different terms and different classifications. Closely linked with these states are the 'Degrees of Prayer' which Happold generalises as the Prayer of Recollection, Prayer of Quiet, and Contemplation Proper. St. Teresa describes four degree of prayer in her *Life* (Chapter II, pp.14-18): here the image is one concerning four kinds of water required to cultivate a garden so that it is to be made for God's pleasure. (F. C. Happold, *Mysticism. A Study and an Anthology*, Harmondsworth, Penguin, rev. ed. 1970, pp.56, 73-77, 342-354.)

8 E. Allison Peers subtitles the various mansions thus: 1st: Humility, 2nd: the practice of Prayer, 3rd: Meditation and Exemplary Life, 4th: the Prayer of Recollection *and also* the Prayer of Quiet, 5th: the Prayer of Union *or* Spiritual Betrothal, 6th: Incipit Union, 7th: the Spiritual Marriage (*Mother of Carmel. A portrait of St. Teresa of Jesus*, London, SCM Press, 1945, 1979, pp.134-141). (See also the scheme outlined in note 7.)

9 Peers, op. cit. pp.131-132. See *The Way of Perfection*, Chapters 20 (based on St. John 14.2) and 28.

10 1st Mansions, Ch. 1, "…we should regard the soul as a castle … in which there are many rooms, just as in heaven there are many mansions." (See also note 9.)

11 Alan Richardson, *The Gospel According to St. John*, London, SCM Press, 1959, etc., pp.164-165; C. K. Barrett, *The Gospel According to St. John*, London, SPCK, 1955, etc., p.381.

12 Barrett, loc. cit. note 11. R. H. Lightfoot paraphrases verse 2: "In His Father's house there is room enough to spare …" (*St. John's Gospel. A Commentary*, London, OUP, 1960, p.209). The verse is surely to be understood in broadly eschatological terms; St. Teresa's use is not eschatological, however, for her spiritual journey and mystical experience is not eschatology as such.

13 W. H. Matthews, *Mazes and Labyrinths. Their History and Development*, London, Longman's, Green, 1922; New York, Dover, 1970, p.193.

14 W. R. Lethaby, *Architecture, Mysticism and Myth*, 2nd. ed., 1892; London, The Architectural Press, 1974, p.163. Dante's Inferno and Paradise involved concentric spheres of nine regions (multiples of three); his Purgatory, however, involved ascent of a mound which had seven 'terraces' of purgation. Lethaby tells us of a seven-walled City of the Dead in the Babylonian Tammuz myth (pp.160-161, 166: the labyrinth is the subject of his Chapter 7, pp.149-173). Death, and the realms of the dead, was clearly central to the Ancient Near Eastern understanding of the labyrinth (see also text below); Lethaby sees a labyrinthine plan beneath the construction of Egyptian tombs (p.169). Though the number seven seems to have come from Ptolemaic cosmology, in later ages it acquired extra symbolic value (see text below).

15 Many versions of the labyrinth myth were connected with the Trojan legends, the searches for maidens carried out by heroes, and the alternative of a labyrinthine descent by both hero or maiden (see Lethaby, work cited note 14, pp.155-156, etc.).

16 See Matthews, work cited note 13, Chapters 10-16; Lethaby, pp.150-151, and Miles Hadfield, *Gardening in Britain*, London, Hutchinson, 1960 etc., pp.54-55. The knot garden, as Hadfield makes clear, was the precursor of the intricate, symmetrical, geometrical *parterre*. The symbolism of the knots would appear to be the opposite of that of the maze or labyrinth, however. Kenneth Woodbridge says: "In mystical thought the maze and knot are related, in that undoing the knot is equivalent to finding the centre; but whereas the maze is open, with a way out, and is therefore an optimistic figure, the knot is closed and pessimistic, expressive of an unchanging or endless situation" ('Rise and decline of the garden knot', *The Architectural Review*, June 1979, p.324).

17 Matthews, p.58, reproducing the suggestion of J. Durand. Lethaby connects (p.164) the floor maze at S. Vitale, Ravenna, with Dante's *Inferno*, Cano XVIII, and quoting lines 4-18.

18 Lethaby. p.162.

19 This is the suggestion of Waldemar Fenn (*Grafica Prehistorica Espana y el Origen de la Cultura Europea*, Mahon, 1950) reported by J. E. Cirlot in *A Dictionary of Symbols*, London, Routledge and Kegan Paul, ET 1962, p.166.

20 Interpretations suggested and reported by J. E. Cirlot (work cited note 19, pp.166-167; sources include Paul Diehl's *Le Symbolisme dans la Mythologie Grecque*, Paris, 1952). Whatever their origin or original meaning, church pavement mazes did acquire more practical uses, namely as routes for symbolic journeys and pilgrimages, in difficult periods when the trip to Jerusalem or Santiago de Compostela was impossible. Concerning labyrinths, mazes, and spirals, in art and religion, see Jill Purce, *The Mystic Spiral: Journey of the Soul*, London, Thames & Hudson; New York, Avon Books, 1974.

21 Another diagram which could represent it is the *mandala*, a pattern built up of concentric rectangles, circles and crosses. The mandala is an image of inner, spiritual, reality, the inner unity of man. Many eastern religious buildings are laid out on a strict mandala plan, particularly certain Buddhist stupas. Such buildings often have a significant ordered progression from thresholds at the perimeter, to the central core where the earth-axis column is represented. Both stupas and early mazes were the object of circumambulation. The mandala may have psychological and cultic connections with the labyrinth.

22 See notes 8 and 7. This becomes apparent when one looks at the treatment of these stages in the text.

23 See Emile Mâle, *The Gothic Image. Relgious Art in France of the Thirteenth Century*, London, Fontana, 1961 (ET of the 1910 French edition), pp.9-10. Numerology, for the Pythagoreans and Medievals, was bound up with geometry, and the most evident testimony to the Medieval skill in geometry is the Gothic cathedral, which *may* have had numerological and symbolic-geometrical formulae built into them; see George Lesser, *Gothic Cathedrals and Sacred Geometry,* London, Tiranti, 1957, particularly Chapter 36, Symbolism. Sacred geometry, and its authentic, original, presence in the fabric of Medieval architecture, and Medieval design intentions, is a much-disputed area.

24 Mâle, work cited note 23, p.11.

25 Three, as we have seen, was a number important to Dante, and was used (text, above) by Juan de Mena.

26 Mâle, work cited note 23, p.11.

27 Ptolemy of Alexandria lived from AD 90 to 168, but his system is based on earlier Greek writers such as Hipparchus (BC 161-126). For the Pythagoreans, "ten was

the mystic number" (Bertrand Russell) – again, the reason behind this is cosmology, for the Pythagoreans calculated ten heavenly bodies, a theory attributed to Philolaus of Thebes (end of the 5th century BC). (Bertrand Russell, *A History of Western Philosophy*, London, George Allen and Unwin, 2nd. ed., 1961, p.223). Ten was, in fact, of little importance in Christian symbolism.

28 See Helen Rosenau, *Vision of the Temple. The Image of the Temple of Jerusalem in Judaism and Christianity*, London, Oresko Books, 1979, pp.94-98, illus. 97-99.

29 According to Nigel Pennick, *Sacred Geometry*, Wellingborough, Turnstone Press, 1980, p.125. It should be noted that Pennick gives no source for this information, and presents many speculations as facts. Helen Rosenau says that Villalpando's (Jerusalem) temple plan has nine courts (work cited note 28, p.95).

30 As an architectural psychologist has put it: "The development of inner layers of personality is cradled in the house, the social structures of marriage and parenthood are nurtured there. It becomes like our clothes, an extension of the self and of the family's personality" (Terence Lee, *Psychology and the Environment*, London, Methuen, 1976, p.65).

31 *Psychology of the House*, London, Thames & Hudson, 1977 (ET of French ed. of 1972), p.7. Marc's ideas appear to owe much to Jungian concepts.

32 Marc, work cited note 31, pp.12-14. He points out that infants from many places and cultures draw the same kind of shape when asked to draw a house – even those who have never seen a house – and often the result resembles a womb-like form (p.12). John Summerson, in his essay 'Heavenly mansions. An interpretation of Gothic' describes the tendency children have to make little houses out of boxes, etc. He suggests that the idea of the little dwelling lies behind certain aspects of the Gothic style (*Heavenly mansions and Other Essays on Architecture*, London, The Cresset Press, 949, p.1-). The archetypal original hut, or primitive hut, is a similar notion, and one that has had a persistent influence in architectural history: see Joseph Rykwert's *On Adam's House in Paradise. The Idea of the Primitive Hut in Architectural History*, New York, Museum of Modern Art, 1972.

33 All these things are true, however, of the House of the Interpreter, in Part I of *The Pilgrim's Progress* (1678). This is a very different piece of architectural imagery, in fact, a series of architectural images. The setting is a very different kind of work, an allegorical story. The house has various rooms where Christian is shown various aspects of the nature of man, his predicament, and the possible means of his salvation. One room depicts the sinful nature of the heart of man, and the Gospel as the only means of cleansing it; another presents Christ and the Devil vying to

sustain and extinguish a fire – the work of Grace in the heart. In a very dark room, a man in a cage symbolises the eternal damnation of unforgivable sin, and in another room, a man dreams of judgement and his unpreparedness. The house and its rooms are obviously straightforward symbols, unlike the complex meanings and functions of St. Teresa's castle.

This article was originally published in the Research Bulletin *of the Institute for the Study of Worship and Religious Architecture (University of Birmingham), 1982, pp.34-42.*

12. Balance

The briefest reading of the gospels, and other parts of the New Testament, shows various very different – contrary, even seemingly-contradictory – things being advocated, and revealed, *at the same time*. Thus it is possible for one person to read it in a way which might make Christianity seem to be very different from that known by someone else's reading; indeed, Christian history has shown how all too easy it is to develop something which is seemingly entirely of one's own making. These different things – different emphases – could be seen as the product of New Testament writers and propagandists promoting what were their own understandings. Equally, they could be placed in the scriptures together – revealed – on purpose, and our job might be that of *holding* them together, accepting the tensions of living with seemingly-contrasting principles. The answer, I consider, is to get the *balance* right – and avoid the natural inclination to try to deny those things, on one side, which don't seem to suit our temperament, or to find reasons, by some casuistry or other, for convincing ourselves that *that* isn't the *real* Christianity, *that* isn't what Jesus really said (we might just blame the Early Church and gospel writers for squeezing it in, with whatever degree of bad motivation we can think of; it's easy to do).

The most obvious tension is between a purely-this-worldly and a next-worldly concern. Time and again, Jesus gives considerable weight to the need to prevent injustice, and bring peace, to *this* world, and his peace is beyond human understanding. In the 'sheep and the goats' story (Matthew Ch. 25) his imperative of love and service – towards people existing in the here-and-now – is sovereign, inescapable and unavoidable, laying a duty upon all of us that has no qualification or limitations. But elsewhere, he makes clear that this thing which he has come to inaugurate – his Kingdom – is *not* of this world. Often we learn that though our conduct must be concerned with *this* world, its ultimate objective is really elsewhere – for this world is 'passing away'. Another tension, of much importance, is related to what I call *communalism*. Jesus is concerned with community, with justly living between people, with simple truth and fairness; Christianity – it has rightly been said – cannot be anything solely about a person's private concerns with their own soul, a spirituality of purely-personal significance. Christ's church exists to serve and create *community*; but to see it in these terms *alone* is to fall into unbalance, to court the disaster of distortion –

for each time Jesus has a personal encounter, he speaks to the very centre of *an individual*. In so many gospel passages, one can see his eyes seeming to bore right through a person to the heart, as he presents them with inescapable choices, requiring decision, action, and total change, from which only the most intransigent will go away sad. Encounter with Jesus (his recorded words alone are sufficient) was always an individual – not a communal – event. A balance we have to strike is between a concern with our self – our destiny – and with others. We must accept the gift of salvation by faith, by Jesus's saving acts; but we must not, thereby, be tempted to ignore the Epistle of James's warning that faith without works is of no avail ("Justification is by faith alone, [Luther is claimed to have said] but faith is never *alone*").

Whenever the right balance is lost, then there is the strong possibility of badness and errors; the classic heresies are precisely these kind of things, where one truth has been exaggerated to the detriment of another, and Jesus's dual nature, human and divine, – the greatest paradox of all – is the tension that became unbalanced in most of them, and very many of our modern distortions are simply, it has been said, new versions of those old kinds of distortion: decrepit, aged sheep in contemporary wolves' designer outfits. One constant imbalance in Christian faith is the overemphasis of reason as against feeling and experience – or the other way around. Try to do without either, and severe problems follow; and today, it is an excess of belief in feeling and emotion which must be curbed, and reason and argument returned. Holding contraries in the right balance is not easy, many fail, perhaps all of us at some time or other; Christianity is far from being the easiest faith to follow, it always contains the pitfall of unbalance, which trips up many; and removing 'difficult' ideas, just to make it simpler for us, can only take us from reality to fantasy.

13. The Spirits About the Throne.
Henry Wilson's Elphinstone Monument, Aberdeen.[1]

The City of Venice – it is not often realised – was extensively bombed during World War I, 42 times between May 1915 and October 1918[2]. Somewhere amidst the wrecked palazzi and roofless churches was a lesser-known, smaller, artistic treasure, or at least potentially so, one – or rather, its pieces – which was hidden for safekeeping until better times, when it might be rescued, and completed. The work in question was the monument to Bishop William Elphinstone (died 1514), founder of King's College (the institution that, along with others, became the modern University of Aberdeen, Scotland); the creator of the monument was English artist Henry Wilson (1864-1934). On Elphinstone's death, he was buried in the chapel of the college which he had created. A monument was later erected, possibly of the late 1590s, adorned with sculpted representations of the Virtues. This was entirely destroyed in religious conflicts, probably in 1639-40, but survives in the form of a written description, or inventory (1542), and other written sources.[3]

The inventory description of the sixteenth century monument speaks of a vested effigy with two angels at the head (carrying candlesticks), and two bedesman (carrying an epitaph) at the feet. On the south side were the three Theological (or contemplative) Virtues (Faith, Hope, and Charity) and also Contemplation, and on the north side, the four Cardinal (or active) Virtues (Justice, Fortitude, Prudence and Temperance) "distinguished by their emblems"; on the east and west sides were the arms of Elphinstone, carried by angels. Ian Campbell speaks of the tomb as "at its most obvious level ... [it was] meant to remind the members of King's College ... in their daily worship in a chapel associated with the [Jerusalem] Temple, that their founder embodied these Virtues and practised an exemplary life, both active and contemplative",[4] and his reconstruction of the monument connects the work with Marian themes, recounting that Elphinstone, in childhood, was inspired by a dream of the Virgin who told him to "apply himself wholly to Virtue" (Boece's *Life* of the bishop was published in 1522), and he devoted his life to serving she who was seen as exemplary in the practice of Virtue/the Virtues. Various contemporary tombs were adorned with sets of the Virtues (eg. that of King Frederick I of Denmark, at Schleswig, 1551-55), but the Elphinstone tomb in addition had the presence of Contemplation, which was not a Virtue, but a goal or climax in the processes of prayer, in which the worshipper has direct knowledge, or perception, of God. Contemplation was also the activity of the cherubim, and the angels who adorned the monument were probably of this kind. They are referred to in Exodus 25; 17-22, where representations are cast in order to be mounted on the Ark of the Covenant, which was later housed in the Holy of Holies of Solomon's Temple. They can also be identified with the four creatures surrounding God, in Ezekiel's vision (1; 4-28 and 10; 8-22), and Virtues and orders of angels were closely identified in early accounts of angelology (eg. Dionysius the Pseudo-Areopagite's *Celestial Hierarchy* of *c.* AD 500). Destruction of this monument, as Campbell suggests, was the loss of a masterpiece, but at least – unlike the majority of losses of Scottish pre-Reformation religious art, the nature and magnitude of which can hardly be ascertained – we know about it due to written records.

In 1891-2, under the principalship of Sir William Geddes, King's College's authorities set about various restorations and adornments of their chapel, and then, after consideration of various options, decided (March 1910) to have the original Elphinstone tomb monument re-created, based on the historic inventory. The resulting work was to be set upon the tomb of the founder: the site of which was discernible (two black marble slabs remained), and became the basis for eventual (extant) re-creation (1931, the slabs being separated by metalwork, etc.) the work of James Cromar Watt. At this time, 1910, the committee, which had been created to oversee production of the work, already had a model before them, produced by Henry Wilson. Henry (or Harry) Wilson trained as an architect, and worked in partnership with the fine Gothicist J. D. Sedding (1838-91), much of whose work he completed (eg. Holy Trinity, Sloane Street, London, 1888-90). His own St. Mark, Brithdir (near Dolgellau, Wales, 1897-1908) is honourably placed among a clutch of Arts & Crafts/Art Nouveau churches in Britain; important, also, are his Byzantinising additions/re-creation of St. Bartholomew, Brighton, 1899-1900. Later in his career he concentrated more on church fittings (eg. the pulpit at Ripon Cathedral, 1912), jewellery, and smaller works. His amazing entry for the Liverpool Cathedral competition (1902, with W. R. Lethaby) recalls Gaudì.

Wilson was chosen because he had already completed work for the University, and had a high reputation among artistic authorities both in the University, and in Scotland; but the story of the monument's creation and eventual unveiling is a long and complex one, with many delays and frustrations, due, perhaps, to the nature of the artist (his perfectionism, financial impracticality, and seeming disregard for the clients and their wishes), and the effects of illness and war upon him. Henry Wilson's usual workshop was at Platt, Borough Green, near Sevenoaks, Kent, and much of the designing was surely done there; in 1912, however, he took a studio in S. Maurizio, Venice, in the artistic atmosphere of which, according to Cyndy Manton, "he felt he could do himself justice as a figure sculptor".[5] Shortly after the monument's eventual unveiling, if not before, a story or myth arose that the artist produced bronzes, in Venice, that were subsequently sunk in a canal, the lagoon, or even the Adriatic itself, when it seemed likely that the Germans would swarm into the city. Certainly, the situation in Venice got so bad that Wilson decided to leave completed work behind, and hastily return to England (he had a young family with him, Manton notes). While the 'submersion of bronzes' theory, the subject of a poem published in Aberdeen in *c.* 1931, was repeated as late as 2009, a more likely possibility, reported by me in 1992, is that plaster casts were buried by Wilson in the garden, and subsequently dug up, and cast in bronze, by Wilson's founder, Munaretti of Murano[6]; the S. Maurizio district (west of St. Mark's Square) seems to have got off comparatively lightly as regards the bombing. Delays continued, and following increasing frustration experienced by the committee in Aberdeen, Professor John Harrower went to Wilson's Venice studio (April 1921), where he was very impressed by the beauty of the bronzes that so far had been cast. Munaretti was given further payments, and casting continued. In April 1924, Harrower visited the foundry itself. As early as January 1914, however, the committee had discovered – they had been sent photographs of casts as they existed then, from Venice – of the essential difference between the sixteenth century monument and its re-created form: the Virtues had Vices sitting beneath them. Warring virtues and vices were an ancient theme in Christian art, and found interpretation in many forms and works, including church wall paintings (eg. those at Claverley, Shropshire, *c.* 1200; as knights on horseback) and Giotto's frescoes in the Arena chapel, Padua (completed *c.* 1305; as standing regal figures, depicted in *grisaille*). The source is the *Psychomachia* of the Spanish poet Prudentius (4th century AD); in the Renaissance, the virtues became transformed into types of learning, mythology, etc.

The monument as Wilson created it is perhaps best understood from his Memorandum of June 1915 (subsequently published in the *Aberdeen University*

Review in 1930-31[7]). In that he wrote: "The arrangement of the Virtues ... is substantially that described in the ancient inventory", however, the origins of the virtues are the "seven creative powers by whom the universe was established ... the seven spirits of God, the seven Elohim ... about the throne ... the sevenfold aspect of divine power" which can be linked to "the sevenfold rhythms and aspects of external nature". He goes on to describe the figures set on the North Side of the monument: "Prudence is really the spirit of order ... seated on the spirit of Rebellion ... she is [thus] shown with compasses setting bounds to the heavens and the earth" and also "calling to Justice, who is order in the moral world and therefore represents knowledge, decision, determination [and is] seated on ... Injustice, which is ignorance. Temperance bears down the dragon of Licence, and ... muzzles him" while holding "the torch of the spirit". ... "Fortitude, strong in suffering, is seated on ... Force, [which is]untamed natural energy. She holds an olive twig to show that only in endurance is peace – this because she is also Meditation, the spirit of communion, the method and means of intuition, inner vision and guidance". On the South Side: "Contemplation [as in the ancient inventory], another aspect of Wisdom ... seated on Folly, [which springs from inattention and] flits thoughtlessly from one subject to another ... Hope, seated on ... Despair, sees what may be a chance of Victory, and is warned by Contemplation to beware lest he strike [with his sword] too hastily and lose the struggle. Hope is also Courage, which is the "root of all the virtues [and is] divine confidence". Next comes Charity ... Mother Love [a mother with child] the feminine aspect of the Godhead. Her hand is laid ... on the knee of Faith, who is Labour, while Hatred [beneath Love, is] self-centred, opposed to spiritual love, [and] bites the heel of the Mother as Eve. Faith or Labour presents the creative aspect of the seven spirits ... and bears the implements and the temporal reward [a money-bag] which ... he hands to Love. [Faith/Labour] is seated on the Basilisk, the emblem of licentiousness and cruelty [and Faith/Labour] typifies the Demiurge, the Creative, everworking Will, inspired by love".

Elohim is the name given to the creator God, used in the early parts of Genesis, and in this thinking that we have described, the act of creation is achieved by means of the presence, within the deity as it were, of the seven creator spirits, identified, as they were/are with the Virtues. Likewise, the hypostatisation Wisdom is, in some accounts, seen as playing a part in Creation. Isaiah names three spirits which will rest upon the 'shoot grown from the stock of Jesse': Spirits of wisdom and understanding, of counsel and power, and of knowledge and the fear of the Lord (11; 1-2). The modern monument, like its predecessor, portrays the lifeless Founder above the virtues, and virtuous life, which he embodies – the sculptures below *point* to his reality and nature – but further, he and his life are identified with the divine Lordship of life and creation that the artist brilliantly embodies and presents.

The first attempt at erecting the Elphinstone monument (siting the bronzes around the Founder's tomb) showed the eventual impracticable nature of the first intentions. The monument was then erected in the ante-chapel in 1931, a crucial contribution being that of Cromar Watt. In 1945, despite disagreement within the University, the monument was re-sited outside the chapel, beyond its west door (and using white marble, not the originally-intended black). I was told, in 2014, that early this century there had been a plan to move the monument back inside, but it had come to nothing.

Of course, I realise that this essay has made no attempt to evaluate or assess the monument in aesthetic or artistic terms, or to seek to describe its stylistic nature and origins; suffice it to say, simply, that Wilson looked to that late-Gothic/early Renaissance synthesis, which produced so many fine tombs and funerary monuments, in the fifteenth/sixteenth centuries. Many other artists/architects in the late-nineteenth/early twentieth century period did so also, producing, for example, the Clarence tomb, Windsor (Alfred Gilbert, 1892-1928), the Gladstone tombs at Hawarden (William Richmond, 1906), the Lever tombs at Port Sunlight (William Goscombe-John, 1913, 1925), the Yeatman-Biggs tomb at St. Michael's, Coventry (Hamo Thorneycroft, 1925), and the Derby monument in Liverpool Cathedral (Giles Gilbert Scott and Thomas Tyrrell, 1908-29)[8] – but the Elphinstone monument is unique in its portrayal of the Virtues, spirits which connect the deceased with the creation and Lordship of the world. And finally, let us not forget that it presents, also, ordinary humans – two servitors – who, perhaps particularly as the result of rainwater staining, seem look out at us resolutely, steadfastly, grimly perhaps, but hopefully.

1 This article makes much use of my detailed study of the monument "The Elphinstone monument at King's College Aberdeen. Its construction in the sixteenth century and reconstruction (1909-31) by Henry Wilson", *Aberdeen University Review*, Vol. LIV, 4, No. 188, Autumn 1992, pp.315-333. It was also published in shorter form in Jane Geddes, ed., *King's College Chapel, Aberdeen, 1500-2000*, Leeds, Northern Universities Press, 2000, pp.245-249 (Ch. 24). I have tried

to keep rigorously to the distinction between an actual *tomb*, and a tomb-like *monument.*

2 G. Scarabello, *Il martirio di Venezia durante le Grand Guerra*, Venezia, Tipographia del Gazzetino Illustratio, 1933, 2 vols. See particularly the photographs, and other information, in volume 1.

3 Ian Campbell, "Bishop Elphinstone's tomb", Ch. 9 in the work edited by Jane Geddes, cited in note 1, pp.115-129. I have made extensive use of this work, both its information about the construction, and regarding meanings, etc. (both much simplified in my account).

4 Work cited note 3, p.125.

5 Cyndy Manton, *Henry Wilson. Practical Idealist*, Cambridge, The Lutterworth Press, 2009, p.116.

6 Manton (location cited note 5) gives Wilson's Venice address as 2778 Calle del Forno, S. Maurizio, but (today at least) S. Maurizio does not seem to have a Calle del Forno; there are at least two thus-named streets in Venice, but they are north and west of S. Maurizio. The bier bears the founder's signature, and the sculptor's ("In Venezia scolpi ..."), and the date 1926.

7 Wilson's June 1915 Memorandum exists in a typescript copy in the Henry Wilson Archive at the Royal College of Art, London, and was published (as "The symbolism") in *The Aberdeen University Review*, 1930-31, pp.216-7, as part of a collection of articles referring to the monument's reconstruction.

8 Concerning the last of these, see John Thomas, "Classical monument in a Gothic church. The memorial to the XVIth Earl of Derby in Liverpool Cathedral", *Transactions of the Historic Society of Lancashire and Cheshire*, Vol. 135, 1986, pp.119-139.

14. Negationism. The Destruction of Western Civilisation.

The history of humanity is the story of mankind's long struggle against the God that created him. This opposition has always been present, and is seen right from disobedience to God's commands, in Eden, right up to the devising of materialist explanations for the emergence of matter and life, a century or so ago – and surely many places in between. In the West, the reaction against the dominance of Christianity, and the world – the civilisation – which it created, has been gaining force since, say, the Eighteenth century, and is presently reaching its climax, with only a little more to go; it will soon be complete. Thus, the culture which we in the West live under, is working hard to negate the principal ideas of the Judeo-Christian tradition. For 'the culture' I often refer to the Rulership – the people who determine things in our world: government, parliament, the judiciary and police, the professions, academia, and, of course – most powerful of all – the mainstream media: we might just say The Establishment or the Elites.

The vital, necessary ideas of the Judeo-Christian world-view are mostly to be found in the Book of Genesis – that is, they come from the beginning. The creation of two – but only two – kinds of people, men and women (2; 15-22); the institution ("in the time of man's innocency" (Book of Common Prayer)) of marriage between one of each (2; 24-5); and the crucial, liberating doctrine known as the Fall, with its vital concomitant, the idea of racial and also personal sin (2, 8-9; 3, 1-24). Today, the creation of the universe, the earth, and all of nature (1, and 2; 1-6) has long been replaced by the materialist (and ludicrous) idea that everything created itself, out of nothing, by chance, undirected, accidental processes. Now, the existence of two sexes (now called 'genders') is being systematically destroyed, and also the essential, inherent, nature of one's sex, and, thus, one's identity. In marriage, sex, and anything concerned with it, the rule now is that *anything* goes, and anything can be (or can be made to be) possible. Above all (in regard to sexual acts) everything exists for one's gratification, and is of necessity beyond one's choice or any free action. Anything can be justified and advocated by use of the simple word 'equality', a concept never seriously examined, referring as it actually does to something in truth impossible between things possessing essential differences (eg. sex).

Belief in the ultimate value of human life, is, of course, a salient victim of materialist negationism, as we drift further and further into the fragile, relativist belief in 'the quality of life', something that can easily be used to justify life's destruction at its beginning, end, and, increasingly, various points between (predicting the future is the most fallible, hazardous human activity of all – but who can doubt that before long the elderly sick, when under-resourced, or lacking 'celebrity status' – ie. worth in purely-this-worldly terms – will be put to death by the state?*) And the destruction of vast amounts of human life – much, much greater than any such destruction in all human history – by the international abortion industry, will one day have consequences, for individuals and society as a whole, of inestimable magnitude. Many will speak of their 'liberating' *intentions*, their utopian desires, but great evil always began as an attempt to make a better world, and meanwhile, the culture of death marches on (already, we should note, having compromised and damaged the medical and 'caring' professions, to say nothing of the law). Meanwhile, the persecution of Christians gains ever more strength (particularly in the Middle East, but its effects move ever nearer); little is done (the churches, for example, seem much more interested in such matters as global warming and relative poverty at home).

The source of much of the badness, and bad events, that invade our Western world is the – utterly groundless – belief, now fully ascendant, in the ultimate *goodness* of people, the idea that people will behave well if treated well, the old idea, which one hears everywhere, of crime being *merely* the result of bad housing and few jobs (of course, this kind of thinking is much more sophisticated than this; and in the wishful-thinking 'hopeful' world of the rulership, it is ubiquitous and unchallengeable). The fact that there was much evil in the past, when this assumption was *not* held, is not relevant, since then, badness came from a different source. Such ideas, and the crime they bring, and allow, are far more acceptable to elitists and 'intellectuals' than the alternative, the utterly dreadful possibility that the theistical world-view might be true, and that *they* might conceivably be subject, ultimately, to some power greater than themselves. Atheism, ultimately, is what some – sadly, influential – people, *prefer to be* the truth or reality (we often hear of the 'radical atheists', but in fact they are *anti*-theists).

Apparently, the student demonstrators at Berkeley, California (early 1970s?) chanted "Western civ has *got to go*!"; their wishes are being granted. The dismantling of Western civilisation certainly does not just concern what might be called the ultimate ideas and values which traditional theology and religious thought assumed; it is also cultural, since there is also a rush to destroy the Western belief in itself and its culture; at its worst, reason itself is regularly undermined, and madness does definitely result (apparently South Carolina has recently passed a law giving its schoolchildren the 'right' to choose not only which sex and sexuality they wish to claim as their identity, but also a choice of which race they 'identify with' as belonging to, and having come from; surgeons in California are apparently now in the act of cutting away the breasts of girls (who suggest that they wish to be boys) as young as *thirteen*). Where people consider they have come from is important, since more and more people are encouraged to disown their past (in some cases, I have heard, people change their surnames, in order to disassociate from the people, and society, that are their actual origins). Certainly, the past is constantly subject to revision, and we regularly see this in television dramas which claim to be set in, say, the 1950s, but whose characters all have 'modern' attitudes (but the past is still sort-of present: they smoke a lot). The media, of course, promote modern art, which is the ultimate de-cultured product (I noticed, when visiting Tate Modern a few years ago, how – to me – depressingly full of people it was: obviously, a work by Rothko or Pollock requires no knowledge, or valuing, of the past unlike that of, say, Titian or Rembrandt, which are totally products of, and imbued with, the narratives and ideas of Classical civilisation and the Bible). The dumbing-down of education, and awareness of the past's rich legacy (and its re-writing so as to depict past existence of a very recent kind of world), plays an important part in negationism, since it makes it so much easier for the rulership to impose its ideas; the next generations are quite without any protection.

Of course, many people, with their honest hopes and good intentions, are ignorant as to the whole that they are part of (many middle-class 'liberals' claim, quite genuinely, never to have heard of Cultural Marxism); it is hard, however, to believe that all are such. Whenever questioned (though this rarely occurs) negationists claim that their 'edited version' of the Judeo-Christian world-view (and Genesis, etc.) *liberates* people – but that is the very last thing it does. Their invisible chains – ever tightening – will be visible one day, a day beyond the possibility of any revision. Eventually, Western civilisation will be replaced by something very different; lucky for those of us who will no longer be around, but those that are will inherit a nightmare.

* I have tried to portray a society – England, in many years' time – where the (Judeo-Christian) values of our civilisation have been totally replaced (a place where they "call evil good and good evil", as Isaiah says; 5; 20), in my novel *Death Tonight*, Twin Books, 2013.

15. Orwell and the Sagrada Familia.

Taste, Culture, & the Valuing of Church Architecture.

English writer George Orwell (1903-1950) famously joined the brigades of foreigners who fought in the Spanish Civil War (1936-9), as told in his book *Homage to Catalonia* (1938). Towards the end of his time in Spain, he returned to Barcelona where he had started, and writes:

> *"For the first time since I had been in Barcelona I went to have a look at the cathedral – a modern cathedral, and one of the most hideous buildings in the world. It had four crenelated spires exactly the shape of hock bottles. Unlike most of the churches in Barcelona it was not damaged during the revolution – it was spared because of its 'artistic value', people said. I think the Anarchists showed bad taste in not blowing it up when they had the chance, though they did hang a red and black banner between its spires." (Chapter XII).*

He is referring, surely, to the Sagrada Familia, the Basilica of the Holy Family, upon which architect Antoni Gaudì (1852-1926) began work in 1883 (it is not, and I fancy never was, Barcelona's cathedral; the first plans for the church were begun slightly before 1883). In the years just after Gaudì's death, I think that only the Nativity transept, with the spires that Orwell refers to, and little else, were built. Today, Gaudì and his work is highly valued, and the large number of visitors to the now-opened interior of the church fund the continued work (a recent TV documentary told of the rush to complete the church in nine years' time (ie. 2026), the large central spires being created with mountains of stone – from Lancashire). Gaudì's work is now often seen as proto-Modern, and the context of Catalan proto-Modernism (eg. the comparable work of Luis Domenech and Francesc Berenguer), along with an early-acquired Medievalism and commitment to Catalan nationalism, are seen as vital in understanding this seemingly-eccentric architect and his work. Few books about Art Nouveau fail to illustrate Gaudì's architecture. To one who studies modern Gothic architecture, the church is very much imbued with Gothic. I would guess that, in the inter-war years, the founders of the Modern Movement, such as Mies van der Rohe and Walter Gropius, would have been less sympathetic to the Catalan than today's Modernists, and even the evaluation of C. R. Mackintosh as a proto-Modernist (as happened early on: *Charles Rennie Mackintosh and the Modern Movement*, Thomas Howarth, 1952), or even a founder of Modernist architecture, would have raised some Modernist eyebrows in the 1920s/30s, steeped, as the great Scotsman clearly was, in various decorative traditions.

The inter-war decades (or rather *c.* 1930 to 1970) were, indeed, the low point in the valuing of historic architecture, decorative traditions, and the stylistic traditions which had come down from the past; and it is easy to imagine that many older or traditionalist-designed buildings were dismal and 'old fashioned' in 1938. (We in Britain had our equivalent, Liverpool Cathedral (1904-80), the campaigns to build the tower and central space of which, must had been conducted in the face of much murmuring). And yet – Orwell reports – the Sagrada Familia was *valued*, and not just for nationalistic reasons (quite who the Anarchists were, I would not know, but presumably one of a number of Left-wing groups opposed to the Fascist forces of General Franco, who at some point held power in Barcelona, when "churches here and there [but not the Sagrada Familia, clearly] were being systematically demolished ..." (*Homage to Catalonia,* Ch. I)). But Orwell did not value it. The idea that one might support destruction of a piece of architecture simply for aesthetic reasons ("hideous"), strikes us as harsh, immoderate – perhaps fanatical – and not a little uncivilised; it brings to mind the recent destruction of ancient religious buildings, in the Middle East, by the Islamic State. Indeed, the Islamist belief, that the world would be a better place when cleansed of the remnants of deceptive pseudo-truth is, arguably, easier to defend than advocating destruction on purely taste grounds. Our view of Orwell, surely, is more often that of a very liberal (in the true sense) and honourable person, albeit not a religious believer or one who might value religious buildings. Other writings by him, I fancy, bestow much value on England and the English countryside, and this presumably must include the English village and its church. It is surely true that, with honourable exceptions, literary people, and maybe many political people, have a certain blindness when it comes to the visual arts (one is used to those who are skilled in mathematics, and the pure sciences, being highly competent and appreciative regarding music, particularly, perhaps, Bach and polyphony – but literary folk and visual art ...?). Many people, particularly of Orwell's generation, would have found, say, modern Gothic architecture, to be 'fake', 'false' or 'pseudo-Medieval', in the bad years cited above (look, for example, at the controversy surrounding the Gothic re-built House of Commons, in 1951) – but would they have been happy with the destruction of such buildings, and would they have imputed *bad* taste, to those who *failed* to commit such destruction?

16. Christianity & Beauty.

A Few Words to Christian Aesthetes.

"I have loved, Oh Lord, the beauty of thy house!* Yes indeed! I have spent most of my life in this rapture – studying and appreciating religious buildings and religious art, swept away by the splendour of church music, and literature, drawn, time and again to paintings and sculpture, and a host of lovely things, both visual and aural – that is, things of the senses – most of which were created in the service of Christian faith – and also writing about them, hopefully with language that honoured and befitted them, and conveyed the splendour (indeed, excitement) that is their essence (I went further, in truth, concerning church buildings, suggesting that they could, by their nature, make possible experiences of an ultimately divine nature). But I am aware that these beautiful things contain danger, both for me, and others like me. Forget the obviously bad things in the world, *good* things, I would suggest, *also* contain hazard (similarly, in the ordering of the world or society: those who have created great evils have very often, I fancy, started out seeking what is good, wanting only to make the world better; passionate well-meaning people are the ones you have to be careful of, for the road to absolute *hell* is paved with very good intentions).

I feel very strongly that the beautiful and good things in the world – works of man, and of nature – all come from God, in their ultimate origins (how many artists have confessed to a strange feeling that they are just *instruments*, or *channels*, merely some means or other whereby goodness, not *originally* of their own making, is brought into the world?); and, perhaps it is thus, that their works *point back* to God, they are the way to reality – Beauty and Truth are, indeed, one, as Keats's Grecian urn tells us. Likewise ugliness, I always think, comes, ultimately, from ... somewhere else, and the fact that some of those who produce it (or is it, for them also, *pro*-creation?) *think* that it is beautiful worries me greatly – but nothing should surprise us in our present former-civilisation. Pursuing beauty must, surely, ultimately, show us truth; but beauty is *not* the only road, and it is a road that can become the way by which people may 'travel hopefully', without any possibility of arriving (arriving at the *only true* destination), indeed, with no wish to arrive, or for anything beyond the ragged glitter of the temporal mirage; never traversing the bridge, they stop, sit down, and feast upon alluring fruit doomed to eventual rottenness, cheerfully ignoring the Bread of Life.

Jesus did not come to bring us beauty: no fine buildings, art, or music, gorgeous apparel, or gold-encrusted altars, were among his promises. Indeed, he tells us that we must reject the things of the world, *even the good things* (which may include the family and its members (Matthew 10, 7-8; Luke 12,51-53); let us always remember Bunyan's Christian, blocking up his ears and running) – and certainly Happiness – if we are fully to follow him, to know Truth. Indeed, he promises us opposition, suffering and the possibility of death as the price of heavenly eternity, and the first disciples experienced this very soon after his resurrection[†]; and it is happening now, at this very moment, perhaps with more severity than even among the tyrannical Romans (not that you would know it from our mainline churches' concerns, or from the media). In the Middle East, large numbers of Christians are regularly put to death by Islamists, and many would have been able to save their lives had they simply renounced Christ. They did not agree to die because of their valuing of beautiful churches or liturgical arts, but because, to paraphrase the words of Graham Kendrick, they loved Jesus more than their own lives. Under Communism, things are just as bad: North Korea has been called the worst place in the world to be a Christian. Of course, no such barbarism (eg the beheading of Egyptian Coptic Christians, by Islamists, in 2015) occurs in the 'enlightened' West; here, the opposition to orthodox Christianity is more subtle, but may well lead in the same direction, in time. Like the Middle Eastern Christians, we may be given a choice: either conforming to the dictates of the state (say, acceding to government coercion regarding pansexuality, school-based sexualisation, evangelistic restriction, or the practices of the Culture of Death), as members of a state-approved Church, fully complying with Establishment so-called 'Christianity' (apparently, at times in the Roman persecutions, Christians would be left alone as long as they worshipped the divine Emperor, and had the required paperwork to prove it), *or* facing criminalisation, such that we would have to worship in secret, perhaps in some former-factories, remote ruins or tattered tower-block flats. Predicting the future is very hazardous indeed, but do not imagine that something like this will *never* happen. Meanwhile, let us enjoy, to the full, the "beauty of thy house", while we can, as long as we know it for what it is, a means – like all the best things in the world – to an end, one means among many, towards the one end – but let it never become an end in itself, or assume the place of an idol – something worshipped *in place of* God.

* "Beauty", here, sometimes causes some confusion. Psalm 25, 8, in the (Roman Catholic) Douai (or Douay) Old Testament, 1609, has "beauty", but most English-language bibles have "the habitation" of God's house (and number it psalm 26), and this includes the Authorised Version/King James Bible, 1611. However, the Old Testament of the New English Bible (Protestant, 1970) has (psalm 26, 8) "O Lord, I love the beauty of thy house", though generally subsequent English translations revert to "habitation" (eg. the New American Standard version, 1977). The Jerusalem Bible (Roman Catholic, 1966) has "I love the house where you live" (Ps. 26, 8). Orthodox bibles use "beauty", apparently, in psalm 25, 8, and this is following the Septuagint, or Greek Old Testament (2nd *c.* AD); the Douai bible came from the Vulgate, or Latin bible (late-4th c.).

† "When Christ calls a man, he bids him come and die." (Dietrich Bonhoeffer, *The Cost of Discipleship*, 1959 edition (London, SCM Press), p.7).

17. Frustration Humour

Some years ago, I saw an old Hollywood film in which two hapless delivery men tried to deliver a piano to a house up many flights of concrete steps; the task was horrendous, nigh-on impossible. We were supposed to find this funny. The film, I now know, was *The Music Box* (1932), and the couple were Laurel and Hardy. I have spent my life trying to get that piano up those steps; I have never succeeded; it was never, as you can imagine, remotely funny. It wouldn't be so bad if such 'humour' were confined to the 1930s – dark days, surely, for many, when there was probably a lot of depression and anxiety in the air, which the film maybe expressed – but the whole genre very much lives on. Time and again, in TV sitcoms for example, we see a hopeless couple faced with an intractable problem, and each action they take makes their situation more and more impossible, and digs them deeper and deeper into a serious mess; and we are supposed to find it funny. Often the initial problem is of their own making (and what about that Hollywood duo? *Surely* they could have phoned on ahead to discover appropriate access? Today's delivery people demand it, sensibly). Such things are awful, just awful. We all have to face terrible frustrations in life, but they are never funny. It makes one think of those poor Danaides, eternally trying hopelessly to fill pierced containers with water (maybe Ovid, or whoever it was, thought that that was a hoot). No, frustration humour is not quite the same as *schadenfreude*, where, more often, a short, simple act or accident causes a misfortune which often has few consequences, and no one could reasonably have anticipated it or caused it; such events rarely lead to an ever-increasing downward spiral of ever-more complex, frustrating, problems.

Not that I'm a humourless sort of chap, far from it. For me, the most satisfying – indeed, incapacitating – sort of humour involves jokes which tell real truth, but whose ends, or punchlines, are unexpected (an elderly male friend recently said to me: "Yes, oh yes, we at home are a very old-fashioned couple, do things the old way, traditional marriage. We discuss a lot of things – but I *always* have the last word ... it's '*Yes*, dear'."). And then there are the times when other people, with all their superior skills and advantages, make a hash of things, which I almost certainly would, like the time in *Galaxy Quest* (1999) – to me, one of the funniest films ever made – when the hapless space-travellers (TV actors, in reality) attempt to launch a space ship out of a docking station, only to scrape the hull against the side (no words needed); such things never happen in *Star Wars* – maybe they should, occasionally. I regularly scrape the side of my space … (well, car). And the sight of Alan Rickman's face, when team 'leader' Tim Allen forces him, yet again, to repeat his mindless TV slogans ("Never give up, never surrender!", "By Grabthar's hammer!") at a boring comic convention, just gives me meltdown; just *thinking* about it renders me incapable of writing. [*Pause dramatique. Intermission*] Another near-wordless piece of hysteria occurs when, in *Chicken Run* (2000), prior to take-off in their improvised plane, the avian 'stewardess' demonstrates use of safety equipment and evacuation procedures, in the familiar fashion, at the front of the plane. And, when take-off is due, the ground grew cry "Chocks away!", and drag from in front of the wheels a couple of Toblerones (triangular chocolate bars). I realise it is more intellectual and a bit precious, but some of the earlier Monty Python sketches were, to me, very funny by way of their use of *verbal equivocation*, as in the *Room For Arguments* ("*Could* be …" "*Might* be …" "*Not* as such …"); I know verbal equivocation does not appeal to many, hence the later, increased popularity of John Cleese's *Fawlty Towers* – but that relied a lot on frustration humour, and had less appeal for me, in consequence.

Did Laurel and Hardy succeed, eventually, with that piano? I never did see the end, since the film had me behind the sofa far more effectively than any Daleks (the worst *they* had in mind was world domination and a few exterminations).

18. Truth

You *don't* believe in truth? Yes you do. It consists of objective reality, that which ultimately *is*, and which is behind everything, and is irrefutable. Of course, people disagree wildly as to what it might be – but that's a completely different thing; ultimately they know, even if they won't admit it, that it's there nonetheless, and it cannot exist (for some people) and at the same time not exist (for others); once, that was obvious: like those who lived in *The Old Vicarage, Granchester*, people once obeyed the Laws of Thought. Now, of course, many consider that we currently live in the age of Postmodernism, we live in a post-truth world – *This is my truth*, they like to say, *now tell me yours*; but they'll come up hard against reality if they seriously try to deny its existence. Find a solipsist, and knee him in the groin (and that reminds me of the philosophy lecturer in my old college who was alleged to doubt his own existence. Once, when walking in the hills – this was Wales – he got truly lost and tired, and, finding a remote phone box – this was long before cell-phones – called a friend of his who owned a car, who might be persuaded to come and pick up the exhausted hillwalker; the friend said: *Where are you? Llanbadarnolwen? Really? Now, you're quite* sure *you're* there ...*? Because if I come all that way to get you, and ...*).

Truth is firmly linked to identity. Despite the occasional depth of sleep, and the seeming-reality of dreams while they're ... in progress, one's own identity is persistent (indeed, persistently so). When we awake, we readily know we're the same entity as we were before, not suddenly transformed into a huge insect (as in Kafka's story), neither are we a completely different person, in a different age, in a different place, with a significantly different body (as in Woolf's novel); sometimes, we might think, it would be not unpleasant being, tomorrow, a Tudor noblewoman; but it never happens. In spring 2017 I had my first general anaesthetic for many years; it was not like sleep; one moment I was there, next I was gone (no dreams), next I was back again; the clocks had curiously moved (and there was a pain in my bleeding foot), but nothing else had changed (just *where* had I been?). Above all, periods of sleep, or anaesthesia, return us – even Woolf's hero/heroine – to personhood, or, indeed, *creaturehood*; Gregor's experience was not so dislocating as we might think: he/it could at least think; tomorrow, the former-me might be a jam doughnut, or a little-known constellation out in the (somewhere) galaxy, or simply a strange hypostatisation of some universal human tendency (such as Hope or Despair); fantasy writers have surely explored all of this.

The universe, and all life, is much like this. It is persistent, and it is regular; it is knowable and it is predictable. It did not come into being by lots of different ways, or the number of different ways in which different people have conceived of its origin. It came about by *one* way; the rest – today, we have to state this quietly, and somewhat apologetically – are *wrong*; the correct one we should call *truth*. If you should return to the *my truth/your truth* people, ask them about the origin of life, and very soon, I'll wager, you have them admitting (alright, it may be reluctantly) to belief in objective truth, to the existence of objective reality (if not, ask them if, like our lecturer, they doubt their *own* existence ... very often ...). If you keep on asking them about the origin of life, and of the possible conclusions, the winding up, of life/the universe/time, eventually, I suggest, you'll come up against the *real* facts of their attitude: they fully accept the conclusions that Science delivers, or allegedly delivers, but remain postmodernist (your truth/my truth/as-many-as-you-like truths) concerning the ideas (which may relate to exactly the same areas of enquiry) put forward by the various *religions* and religious philosophies. It's fully respectable (in popular thought, and thought of many kinds) to be post-truth (dismissive of the concept of objective reality) when it comes to ideas found in religions, but science (ie. the popular, lay, idea about What Science Says) – is very different; no room for disagreement *there*, oh no, no, no; not long ago, I saw a popular television scientist reel off a list of things YOU HAVE TO believe).

"No problem – [your truth-doubter might say] religions have their stories about origins and ends, but they're just stories; they make no *truth*-claim, they're not about objective reality [Ah! So you *do* believe in it!]". This is where I differ. Christianity (I have no information or opinion regarding other religions) does indeed make truth-claims: nowhere in the recorded words of Jesus, or other New Testament writers such as St. Paul, is there even a hint that the ideas about reality, which their words state or imply, might be treated as *partially* true, *one way* of looking at the truth, or the way certain people (like Judaic believers) might look at truth, but not (with equal validity) others. Christianity is not modernist or postmodernist. It has been said (against the idea that Jesus's death and resurrection was a fraud devised by the apostles and the Early Church) that no movement – if we agree to call it such – could have been raised upon ideas which were *known* to be false; likewise, a movement could not have been developed and sustained by a group which believed it had not come to possess *the* truth (the first martyrs, or the many who are suffering hideously for the Christian faith right now in many parts of the world, could only endure torture and death for something that was really *really* true); and certainly, a religion, church organisation, or denomination, which claimed it had only a part of the truth would not last very long, and would quickly be replaced by one that did; I fancy we are seeing this process take place at the present time. Other people concede that, yes there is such a thing as truth – but (they argue) "different people have different *interpretations* of what it really is" (they're not talking about scientific ideas); this, I consider, is a return of the postmodernist you truth/my truth, in a slightly concealed form (you wouldn't have got people in the pre-Modern era dissembling like this).

Of course, there are people who prefer to go on continuously searching; 'Better to travel hopefully than to arrive' – is their watchword. In fact, they are more likely to be travelling *hopelessly*, since the endless travelling becomes an end in itself, an obsessive substitute for any conclusion or destination, and they might be actually going round and round and round in circles (a version, perhaps, of Sartre's *Huis Clos*); indeed, they may – to change the metaphor – be like mere grass blowing in the wind. Such a thing is not unpleasant, necessarily, and probably more pleasant than actual commitment; they dismiss those who do arrive at a destination and commit themselves to a truth, as 'absolutists', recalling those unpleasant European monarchs of a few centuries ago. In fact – pleasant though it may be – the totalitarianism that they have blindly, but not entirely innocently, entered into is the 'tyranny of relativism', which Pope Benedict warned of; and relativism, currently, rules our world (well, the West). But their endless searching – reading book after book, each with its different 'radical' ideas, sitting endlessly at the feet of a new sage or guru who promises something enlightening – is not to be confused with perpetual questioning, doubting and scepticism, which, I argue, is a vitally-necessary process, and leads eventually to orthodox Christianity (particularly if the questioning includes scepticism regarding the whole process, method, and nature of the intense questioning that orthodox Christian ideas – but not others – were subjected to in recent decades).

I read recently that Jesus came to earth at the absolute right time (it was planned that way – "God knows what he is about", as I fancy J. H. Newman wrote); this has always been my view, since the worst thing that can happen to the truth that may set us free is that we should in any way be *compelled* to accept it – as would be the case if it had been revealed in a time when modern methods of validating truth (scientific, historical, legal, etc.) had been available (YOU HAVE TO believe…). Jesus's truth is always definite and non-negotiable: but he often experienced people who chose to reject it; acceptance was thus a free, individual act, requiring commitment (and often came at a cost, as it does now). A brief survey of the 'miracles' he performed shows clearly that even they did not *compel* assent to his implied world-view, truth claims, or his clearly-stated information as to his own identity (as in C. S. Lewis's assessment, we should not expect a committed atheist to be at all swayed by experiencing a miracle). This element of free choice and commitment indicates to us that there is much accuracy in the oft-suggested idea that the rot started to set into Christ's Church when Christianity became the official religion of the state, with acceptance eventually becoming a fact of coercion (by the culture, and by the Establishment, the civil law). Of course many people, in the centuries of Christendom, possessed personal commitment; but many did not.

It may be suggested that the fullest truth – everything about everything – is greater than the human mind is capable of understanding, or knowing, and that therefore no one (religious people, scientists, philosophers) can know *everything*. Some people deny this, saying that reason shows us that things which are inconceivable, by us, must remain beyond the bounds of possibility, beyond the realm of *everything* or *something*; they may be right, but if they are not, then religious people might conceivably say that they have been told – above all, religion is about what has been *revealed*, above and beyond the (perfectly valid) products of human reason – all that the human mind is capable of grasping, or all that they are required to know, and that their knowledge is not, therefore, that which can not be called fullest *truth*, and that if, in a future (non-this-worldly) state, they 'learn' more, this does not negate the *whole* truth of the this-worldly revelation. Certainly, if Christianity is not first and foremost concerned with truth, and possesses truth, then it is useless to all, or rather worse, it is pure deception that could divert us from reality, and the search for it.

So all one has to do, now, is to work out exactly what the truth about everything is, and commit ourselves to it, to prioritise this search before all other human quests (and all other human concerns). This will not be easy, but claiming that there is, or might be, no ultimate truth to be looked for, is an evasion of what is our only real duty in this life – *this* quest is certainly the only thing in this life that matters, or that will have eternal consequences; and evading it may cost us dearly. Finding truth, pursuing truth, serving truth, I would argue, is more important than trying to find happiness.

By John Thomas

Redemption Achieved. John Singer Sargent's *Crucifixion of Christ with Adam & Eve* and its place in his work

Sargent's sculpture of Christ's crucifixion was created to form the centrepiece of the "Christian end" of the mural cycle *The Triumph of Religion,* with which the artist decorated part of Boston Public Library, a cycle which took him from 1890 and remained unfinished in 1917.

In addition to the plaster and wood relief *in situ* in Boston, Sargent commissioned a series of bronze casts of his work, large (life-size figures; St. Paul's Cathedral, London), medium (Tate Gallery, London, and Fogg Museum, Massachusetts), and small (which were given to friends, and are now mostly in public collections). This little book is the first major study of this important *fin de siècle* work. The Foreword is by Richard Ormond, the foremost Sargent scholar.

Death Tonight

A place to be travelled through very quickly, without stopping, is the England of the late-21st century – in which human conceptions are reprocessed by the State, lifespans are limited by "usefulness", the ubiquitous Care Bureau reports on everyone and everything – and TV gameshows are truly deadly affairs. Carry (D659803) a fugitive *lolly,* Ann'a the underground *proddy-puller,* and illicit *product* Frang, are escaping from the vicious Commander Ronammo, with the help of Gerde the fowl-bargee, Ann'a's young apprentice Fid., and tintinabulist twins Yayan and Yuan. But the Rulership, in their secluded, luxurious apartments – Haamun, and his all-obliging pet Onesimus, Guerlock, Director of the State Security Service, and, Governor of all, the pale, chilling, Brumis – live a *very* different kind of life ...

Not Long Now

Now confined to a care home, tragic, failed painter Robert Levenham is physically bound by his circumstances, and the effects of his dementia – but that doesn't stop his mind ranging over the ideals and efforts of his life, and the previously-hidden knowledge that beneath the calm exterior of his work, lay another secret of a strange, unsuspected kind. When embarking on her first research project, novice art historian Daisy Taylor never imagines that she will encounter family revelations, motiveless aggression, and personal danger – and discover more than she bargained for about her own precarious origins.

Set mostly in St. Ives, Cornwall – a town long known for its artists and their work – *Not Long Now* explores the meaning and purpose of a person's life, when looked back on, beneath the outer façade of the commonplace identity that everyone knows and sees.

Beyond This Wilderness

Two present-day Shropshire clergymen discover a document explaining why, in the 18th century, members of the local landowning family fell victim, one by one, to a curse whose effects ravage their bodies and destroy their minds. But the source of the evil is not in the least something consigned to former times ... The "Testament" had been produced, and secreted, by the village parson, and was intended to explain the nature and source of the badness, for those who might experience it in later times – and also, unintentionally, it reveals the faith and hope that might lead us all to the "milk and honey" that lie beyond the wilderness of this world.

Christianity and Materialism. The Church, And the World, In Western Society

This spirited defence of orthodox Christianity locates the faith's ills and problems, not in recent dissentions and controversies, but in the results of Western civilisation's turning to materialist philosophies and world-views in the later nineteenth century, the result of the ascendance of evolutionism, and all its products and implications. Only Christians' direct rejection of materialist worldviews and their foundation – the author argues – can restore society to a true, wholesome and balanced state.

The Welsh Dresser & Various Tails

The ultimate mystery of another person's life; the myths, and realities, of the creative artist; the ineluctable process from desiring freedom towards exercising power; the nightmarish future reality we all risk; the possibilities of past misdemeanours, and regrets, coming to re-visit us – these are just some of the themes found in this highly original collection of stories.

Department E

" '*Enabling Society to Fulfil Its Potential*' – that, Mr Jones, is my Department's mission, and its *potential* is very great." "The most *fulfilled* society is that in which the individual realises his own potential *beyond all others!*"

Trapped in a tunnel after an explosion, a young man called Jones stumbles upon what appears to be the offices of a – literally – underground organisation. Assuming this to be a secret government department or military installation, he expects to be interrogated, then eventually released. To his surprise, he finds himself being lectured and harangued, for many days on end, by the strange, but polished and urbane person who appears to be in charge of the place, who only identifies himself as the "Chief Executive". Escaping, Jones is helped by a not-so-ordinary secretary, Silverthorne, with whom he eventually finds himself in a Victorian castle on the Welsh coast, and there discovers the full import and significance of the way by which C. E.'s department – and its dreaded Director – seek to impose their will on the human race.

Benebella

"Beauty is experienced, but the experience can go beyond the things of the eyes and the senses, towards joy and goodness. Goodness leads on to charity and love ...". A painting entitled *Benebella* is found in a dusty second-hand shop in a back-street of Edwardian London, and it has a curious effect on the young insurance clerk, Abel Smythe, who finds it there... *Benebella* is a portrait whose beauty inspires acts of goodness and philanthropy. Unlike Dorian Gray's picture, however – in Oscar Wilde's classic tale – the more *Benebella's* owner does good works, the more disfigured and ravaged the picture becomes – in a story which overturns the amoral aestheticism of Wilde's character, and the corrupting hedonism of J-K Huysmans' Duc des Esseintes, upon whom Wilde drew. Beauty, goodness, and the moral nature of art, are interrelated in this period-piece novella.

Available (print and electronic) from the Twin Books website – www.twinbooks.co.uk

CW01647360

L'ESCOLA de MONSTRES

JA CONEIXES TOTS ELS MONSTRES?

APRENDRE A LLEGIR

- a -

L'ESCOLA de MONSTRES

Il·lustracions de CHRIS KENNETT

SALLY RIPPIN
Adaptació de JÚLIA COT

UNA MASCOTA TRAPELLOTA

montena

ATURA'T, NO FACIS CAP DISBARAT!
ÉS MILLOR QUE DEIXIS EL LLIBRE TANCAT!

CAL QUE ESTIGUIS BEN ALERTA...

L'ESCOLA de MONSTRES JA ÉS OBERTA.

EL PROFESSOR TOCA LA CAMPANA.

SOM-HI, COMENÇA LA SETMANA.

TOTS EN FILA
ESPEREN ENTRAR.

DESPRÉS DE CLASSE PODRAN JUGAR.

AVUI ÉS UN DIA
MOLT ESPECIAL:

DILLUNS DE MASCOTES, I AIXÒ ÉS GENIAL!

PRIMER LES MASCOTES HAN D'ESMORZAR.

SI TENEN GANA
NO PODEN PASSAR.

ELLA L'AMAGA
DINS DEL BARRET.

I SEU A L'ESTORA
COM SI NO PASSÉS RES.

AVUI APRENDRAN
A COMPTAR FINS A DEU.

ON ÉS EL LLAPIS,
ALGÚ D'AQUÍ EL VEU?

S'HO MENJA TOT,
AQUESTA MASCOTA.

NO PARA DE CRÉIXER
I ÉS BEN TRAPELLOTA.

L'ANIMALÓ DEVORA
I DEVORA.

FINS I TOT,
S'EMPASSA L'ESTORA.

–S'HA MENJAT LA MEVA PERRUCA!

MAI NO EN TÉ PROU,
VOL MÉS MANDUCA.

—MARIA, ESTÀ FORA DE CONTROL!

ATURA'L
O ES CRUSPIRÀ
EL SOL!

CORRE FELIÇ PERQUÈ S'HA ESCAPAT.

PERÒ EL JARDINER
HA CAVAT UN FORAT.

ÉS UN FORAT GROS
I PROFUND.

PER ATRAPAR-LA
JA ESTÀ TOT A PUNT.

ARA UNA XARXA. CREIEU QUE HA FUNCIONAT?

SÍ! ENTRE TOTS DOS L'HAN CAPTURAT!

TATXAAAN!

—NO VULL MÉS MASCOTES A L'ESCOLA!

—NO PATEIXIS,
NO ET DEIXARÉ SOLA.

HA SIGUT DIVERTIT,
TANT ENRENOU.

POTSER UN ALTRE DIA
LA HI PORTA DE NOU.

APRÈN PARAULES NOVES
ENTRAR
OBERTA
DISBARAT
ALERTA
AL LLARG DEL LLIBRE AQUESTES PARAULES ESTAN ESCRITES EN COLOR BLAU. LES RECORDES?
PARAULES NOVES:
NIVELL FÀCIL
NIVELL DIFÍCIL
JUGAR
GENIAL
DEVORA

SETMANA

RES

PASSAR

ESPECIAL

ESTORA

PERRUCA

MASCOTA

DEU

FORAT

CAMPANA

TRAPELLOTA

ENRENOU

SOLA

NOU

ESMORZAR

MANDUCA

VEU

PROFUND

CAPTURAT

FUNCIONAT

BARRET

CONTROL

TANCAT

A PUNT

ESCOLA

ESCAPAT

SOL

COM ES FA SERVIR AQUEST LLIBRE

Aprèn a llegir a l'Escola de Monstres!

Als infants els encanta escoltar els adults llegir en veu alta. Llegir i explicar-los històries des de ben petits és la millor manera perquè associïn els llibres amb una experiència divertida i es familiaritzin amb el llenguatge.

TRUCS I RECURSOS PER GUIAR I MILLORAR LA LECTURA

- Comenteu junts les imatges, que us expliquin què hi veuen.
- Quan llegiu en veu alta, aneu seguint el text amb el dit, d'esquerra a dreta.
- Podeu anar assenyalant les paraules destacades en verd i ensenyar-los com es pronuncien.

- A mesura que agafin confiança, atureu-vos en aquestes paraules i animeu-los que les llegeixin i les pronunciïn sense la vostra ajuda.

- Després podran tornar a practicar aquestes paraules gràcies a la llista que hi ha al final del llibre.

Ja veureu com, a poc a poc, els petits lectors es veuran capaços de llegir tots sols i qui sap si, també, d'inventar les seves pròpies històries de monstres.
Visca la imaginació!

Sally Rippin és una de les escriptores infantils més estimada i reconeguda de tot el món. Ha escrit una cinquantena de llibres per a infants i joves i ha obtingut un munt de premis. Les seves obres més destacades són *Billie B. Brown, Hey Jack!* i les sèries Polly i Buster. A la Sally li agrada escriure històries emotives i crear personatges amb qui tant els petits com els pares i els professors es puguin identificar.

WWW.SCHOOLOFMONSTERS.COM

COM ES DIBUIXA LA MARIA

① Amb un llapis, dibuixa un triangle alt i estret.

② Afegeix-hi tres triangles petits perquè et quedi la forma d'un barret. Esborra les línies que se solapin.

③ Dibuixa un cercle per fer el cap, un rectangle que s'eixampli per fer el cos i dos quadrats petits per als peus.

④ Dibuixa dos cercles per fer els ulls i els botons del vestit. Fes un puntet dins de cada ull i dues cuetes per als cabells.

(5) Fes uns dibuixets en forma de U, que seran les orelles, el nas i la boca. Afegeix-hi un parell de tires allargades per fer els braços.

(6) Per acabar, només faltarà incloure-hi les mans, els peus i els detalls que vulguis. Ah! I no t'oblidis de l'aranya!

Chris Kennett dibuixa des que és capaç d'agafar un llapis (o almenys això explica la seva mare). Fa més de vint anys que es dedica professionalment a dibuixar personatges extravagants. És conegut mundialment per dissenyar les estranyes i meravelloses criatures de *Star Wars*, però també li encanta dibuixar monstres tendres i adorables com els d'aquest llibre... I li agradaria que tu també ho fessis!

ESCOLA de MONSTRES

HAS LLEGIT TOTS ELS LLIBRES DE LA COL·LECCIÓ?

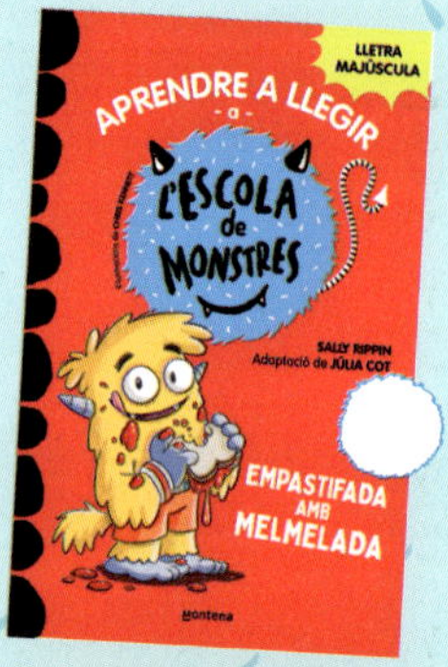

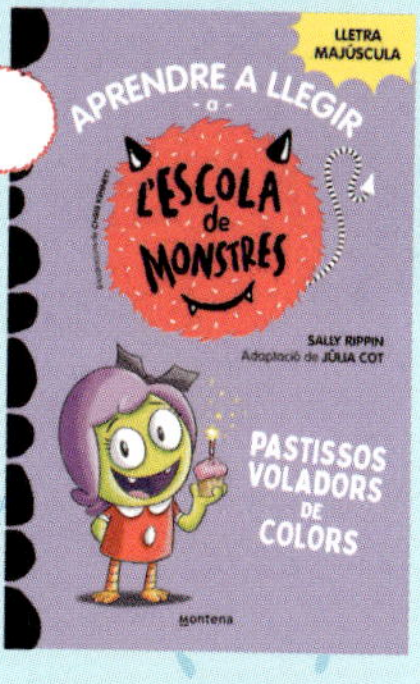
LLETRA MAJÚSCULA
APRENDRE A LLEGIR
a
L'ESCOLA de MONSTRES
SALLY RIPPIN
Adaptació de JÚLIA COT
PASTISSOS VOLADORS DE COLORS
Montena

LLETRA MAJÚSCULA
APRENDRE A LLEGIR
a
L'ESCOLA de MONSTRES
SALLY RIPPIN
Adaptació de JÚLIA COT
MALIFETES BEN FETES
Montena

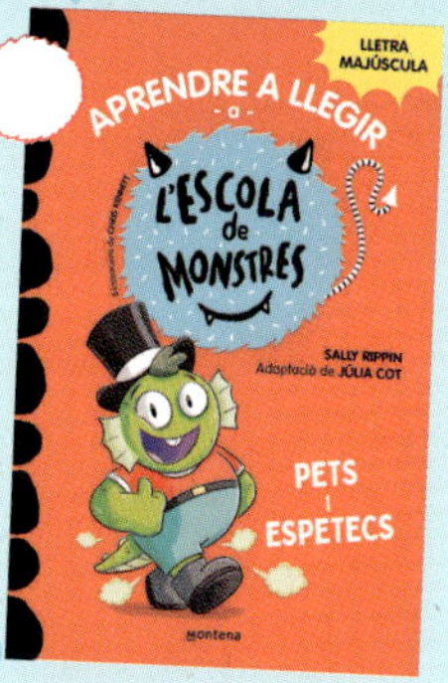
LLETRA MAJÚSCULA
APRENDRE A LLEGIR
a
L'ESCOLA de MONSTRES
SALLY RIPPIN
Adaptació de JÚLIA COT
PETS I ESPETECS
Montena

LLETRA MAJÚSCULA
APRENDRE A LLEGIR
a
L'ESCOLA de MONSTRES
SALLY RIPPIN
Adaptació de JÚLIA COT
EMOCIONS DE COLORS
Montena

LLETRA MAJÚSCULA
APRENDRE A LLEGIR
a
L'ESCOLA de MONSTRES
SALLY RIPPIN
Adaptació de JÚLIA COT
SAPASTRE I BONASTRE
Montena

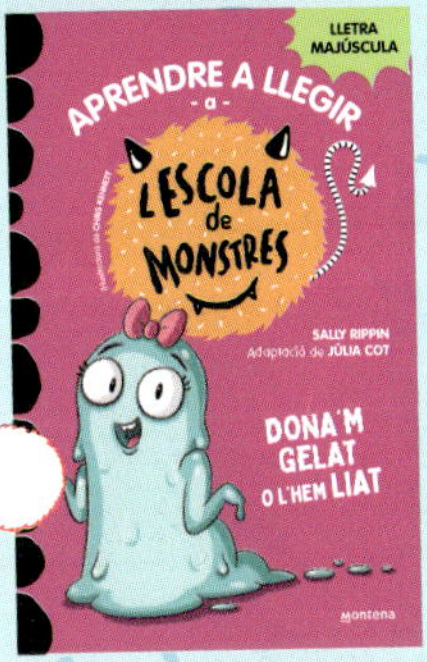
LLETRA MAJÚSCULA
APRENDRE A LLEGIR
a
L'ESCOLA de MONSTRES
SALLY RIPPIN
Adaptació de JÚLIA COT
DONA'M GELAT O L'HEM LIAT
Montena

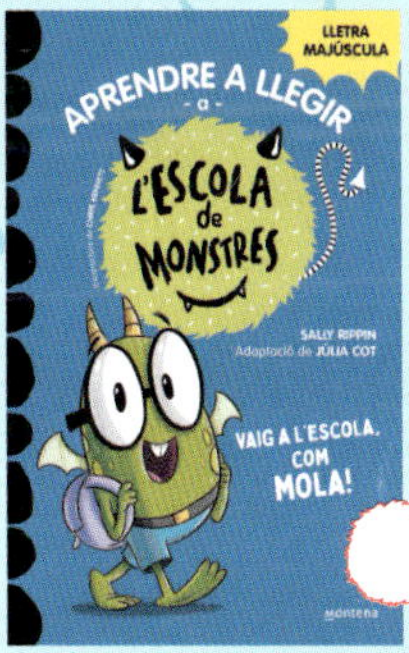
LLETRA MAJÚSCULA
APRENDRE A LLEGIR
a
L'ESCOLA de MONSTRES
SALLY RIPPIN
Adaptació de JÚLIA COT
VAIG A L'ESCOLA, COM MOLA!
Montena

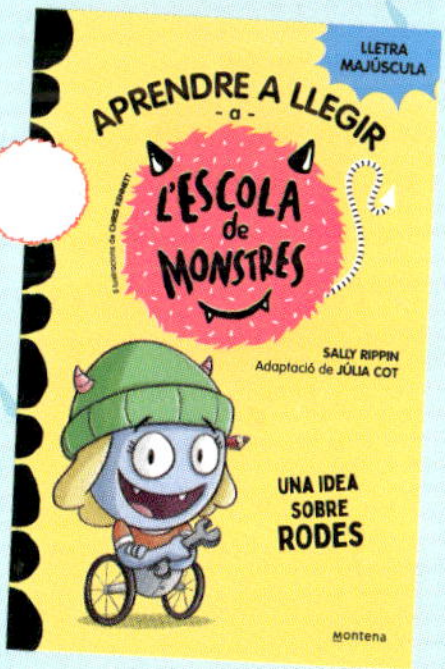
LLETRA MAJÚSCULA
APRENDRE A LLEGIR
a
L'ESCOLA de MONSTRES
SALLY RIPPIN
Adaptació de JÚLIA COT
UNA IDEA SOBRE RODES
Montena

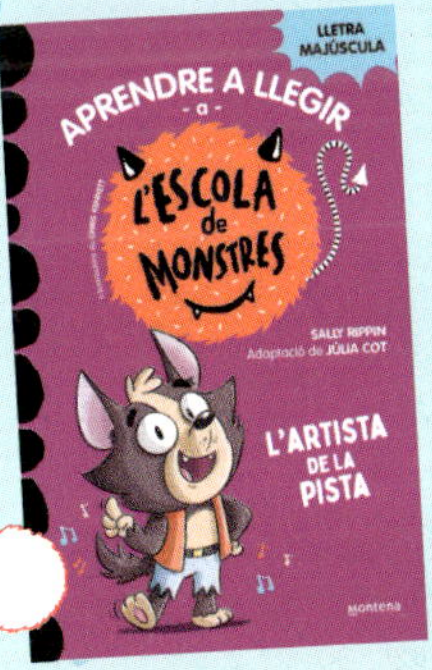
LLETRA MAJÚSCULA
APRENDRE A LLEGIR
a
L'ESCOLA de MONSTRES
SALLY RIPPIN
Adaptació de JÚLIA COT
L'ARTISTA DE LA PISTA
Montena

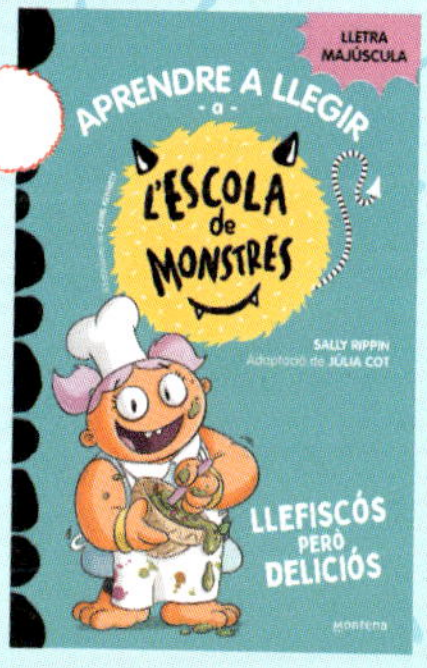
LLETRA MAJÚSCULA
APRENDRE A LLEGIR
a
L'ESCOLA de MONSTRES
SALLY RIPPIN
Adaptació de JÚLIA COT
LLEFISCÓS PERÒ DELICIÓS
Montena

LLETRA MAJÚSCULA
APRENDRE A LLEGIR
a
L'ESCOLA de MONSTRES
SALLY RIPPIN
Adaptació de JÚLIA COT
AFAMADA I ENFADADA
Montena

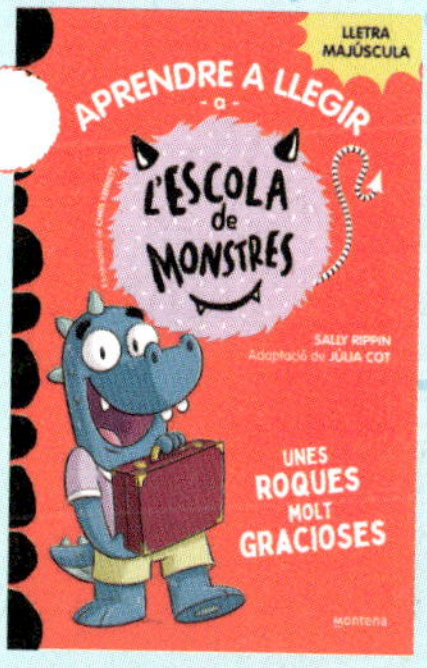
LLETRA MAJÚSCULA
APRENDRE A LLEGIR
a
L'ESCOLA de MONSTRES
SALLY RIPPIN
Adaptació de JÚLIA COT
UNES ROQUES MOLT GRACIOSES
Montena

Paper certificat pel Forest Stewardship Council®

FSC www.fsc.org
MIXT
Paper | Donant suport a la silvicultura responsable
FSC® C117695

Penguin Random House Grupo Editorial

Títol original: *Mary Has the Best Pet*
Primera edició: març del 2022
Onzena reimpressió: octubre del 2024

© 2021, Sally Rippin, pel text
© 2021, Chris Kennett, per les il·lustracions
© 2021, Hardie Grant Children's Publishing, pel disseny de la sèrie
Publicat per primera vegada a Austràlia per Hardie Grant Children's Publishing
Drets negociats a través d'Ute Körner Literary Agent - www.uklitag.com
Tots els drets reservats, inclosos els drets de reproducció total
o parcial en qualsevol forma.
© 2022, Penguin Random House Grupo Editorial, S. A.
Travessera de Gràcia, 47-49. 08021 Barcelona
© 2022, Júlia Cot, per la traducció

Penguin Random House Grupo Editorial està a favor de la protecció de la propietat intel·lectual. La propietat intel·lectual estimula la creativitat, defensa la diversitat en l'àmbit de les idees i el coneixement, promou la lliure expressió i afavoreix una cultura viva. Gràcies per comprar una edició autoritzada d'aquest llibre i per respectar les lleis de propietat intel·lectual en no reproduir ni distribuir cap part d'aquesta obra per cap mitjà sense permís. En fer-ho esteu donant suport als autors i permetent que PRHGE continuï publicant llibres per a tots els lectors. De conformitat amb el que disposa l'article 67.3 del Reial decret llei 24/2021, de 2 de novembre, PRHGE es reserva expressament els drets de reproducció i d'ús d'aquesta obra i de tots els seus elements a través de mitjans de lectura mecànica i altres mitjans idonis amb aquesta finalitat. Dirigiu-vos a CEDRO (Centre Espanyol de Drets Reprogràfics, http://www.cedro.org) si necessiteu reproduir algun fragment d'aquesta obra.

Printed in Spain – Imprès a Espanya

ISBN: 978-84-19085-33-7
Dipòsit legal: B-880-2022

Compost a El Taller del Llibre, S. L.
Imprès a Gómez Aparicio, S.L.,
Casarrubuelos (Madrid)

GT 8533B